THE PICTORIAL HISTORY OF THE
SWORD

THE PICTORIAL HISTORY OF THE
SWORD

A DETAILED ACCOUNT OF THE DEVELOPMENT OF SWORDS, SABRES, SPEARS
AND LANCES, ILLUSTRATED WITH OVER 230 PHOTOGRAPHS AND ARTWORKS

HARVEY J S WITHERS

southwater

PICTURE CREDITS
The publisher would like to thank the following for kindly supplying photos for this book: Alamy: 53br, 62bl, 83tr; AKG: 15br, 16bl, 18bl, 22tl, 26bl, 28tr, 31br, 35t, 36br, 37tr, 43br, 60tl, 93tr; Ancient Art & Architecture: 17tr, 88tr; The Art Archive: 16tr, 20br, 21t, 23b, 48b, 59tl; Berman Museum of World History, Alabama: 7b, br, 9tr, 10br, 11b, 12t, 57bl, 64t, t, b, 65m, 79b, 81br, 85b, 88br, 90t, 91b, 93b, 94b; Bridgeman Art Library: 7tl, tr, 13m, 14bm, 21b, 24b, 27tr, 28br, 29tr, bl, 32tl, 40tl, 43tl, 44bl, 46tl, 50t, bl, 51tr, 57br, 58bl, 69mr, 73mr, 84bl, 89tr, 90bl; Corbis: 10t, 56mr, 109b, 78b; Getty Images: 77ml, 79tr, 85tr; Hermann Historica Auctioneers, Munich: 19tl, 19tm, tr, br, bl, 38t, b, 41t, mr, b, 80b, 86tm; Michael Holford: 15tr, 100tl, m; iStock: 171br; Jean Brink: 69tl, br; Jupiter Images Corporation: 15tl, 17br, 25tr, 30tl, 52tl, 55tl, 65tr; David Xavier Kenney, South Beach FL (www.RomanOfficer.com): 22bl, 23tr; TopFoto: 23ml, 45br, 47t, b, 67mr, 76tr, 88tr, 89bl, 91t, 92tr, bl; Harvey Withers: 60b, 63b, 73b, 75t. All other images from the Royal Armouries, Leeds in England. All artwork by Peters & Zabransky Ltd.

This edition is published by Southwater

Southwater is an imprint of Anness Publishing
Hermes House, 88–89 Blackfriars Road, London SE1 8HA
tel. 020 7401 2077; fax 020 7633 9499
www.annesspublishing.com www.southwater.com
© Anness Publishing Ltd 2010

If you like the images in this book and would like to investigate using them for publishing, promotions or advertising, please visit our website www.practicalpictures.com for more information.

ETHICAL TRADING POLICY
Because of our ongoing ecological investment programme, you, as our customer, can have the pleasure and reassurance of knowing that a tree is being cultivated on your behalf to naturally replace the materials used to make the book you are holding. For further information about this scheme, go to www.annesspublishing.com/trees.

UK distributor: Book Trade Services; tel. 0116 2759086; fax 0116 2759090; uksales@booktradeservices.com; exportsales@booktradeservices.com
North American distributor: National Book Network; tel. 301 459 3366; fax 301 429 5746; www.nbnbooks.com
Australian distributor: Pan Macmillan Australia; tel. 1300 135 113; fax 1300 135 103; customer.service@macmillan.com.au
New Zealand distributor: David Bateman Ltd; tel. (09) 415 7664; fax (09) 415 8892

Previously published as part of a larger volume: *The Illustrated Encyclopedia of Swords and Sabres*

A CIP catalogue record for this book is available from the British Library.

Designed and produced for Anness Publishing by
THE BRIDGEWATER BOOK COMPANY LIMITED.
Publisher: Joanna Lorenz, Editorial Director: Helen Sudell
Project Editor: Sarah Doughty
Photography: Gary Ombler (Armouries) and David Cummings (Berman)
Designer: Alistair Plumb, Art Director: Lisa McCormick
Production Manager: Christine Ni

With special thanks to the Royal Armouries, in Leeds, England, and the Berman Museum of World History, in Anniston, Alabama, USA. Also grateful thanks for the assistance of Hermann Historica Auctioneers, Munich.

Publisher's Note: Although the advice and information in this book are believed to be accurate and true at the time of going to press, neither the authors nor the publisher can accept any legal responsibility or liability for any errors or omissions that may be made.

Page 1: Crusader knight. Page 2: The Relief of the Light Brigade at the Battle of Balaklava, 25 October 1854. Page 3: Napoleon at the Battle of the Pyramids, 21st July 1798. Page 4: Norman troops, Bayeux Tapestry. Page 5: (Top) Fencing, from 'Tacuinum Sanitatis'. (Bottom) Lieutenant Frederick Robertson Aikman at Lucknow, the Indian Mutiny, 1 March 1858.

Contents

Introduction

From the primitive edged weapons used by early humans through to those of the modern world, the history of the sword covered in these pages is a truly fascinating story. It has been used as a fighting weapon, a symbol of authority, a mark of social rank and as a ceremonial object. For centuries, the sword remained the first weapon of choice for the military soldier and its pre-eminence was secured by a combination of continuous technological improvements and adaptation to ever-changing battlefield conditions.

Early swords and sabres

We begin this book by looking at the historical background to the development of edged weapons and an examination of the simple tools of Stone Age people, including hand-held flint points and the first axes, which date from 1.4 million years BC. We then move ahead in time to focus on such ancient civilizations as Sumeria and Mesopotamia, where metalworkers began to combine bronze and copper alloys to produce reliable spears, axeheads and swords.

In ancient Egypt, the countless invasions and subsequent assimilations led to the introduction of bronze- and iron-bladed weapons. Although noted for their reliance on the spear and shield, the Greek infantryman or "hoplite" also carried a straight, double-edged, leaf-shaped short sword known as the "xiphos" and it became the model for the more recognizable Roman "gladius". At this time, Celtic swordsmiths were also producing swords of unique beauty and robustness.

11th- to 17th-century European swords

In Europe, the wide-bladed and double-edged Saxon and Viking broadsword would become the inspiration for the early medieval "knightly" sword of the 11th to the 14th century. In both Europe and Asia, polearms (pole-mounted weapons) were used on the battlefield,

ABOVE At the Battle of Agincourt, October 1415, French knights launched an attack on an exhausted and much smaller English army, but were beaten back by the fearsome longbows of the English and Welsh.

and in the jousts of the medieval and Renaissance periods, public displays of horsemanship and fighting skills were performed using the lance and the sword.

Sword design changed during the Renaissance and, from around 1400, the emphasis shifted from a sword that had cutting and slashing capabilities to one that could pierce plate armour. Around 1500, the rapier appeared and soon became the sword of choice for a gentleman and the ultimate weapon for trials of honour, such as the duel. German and Swiss mercenaries ("Landsknechte") roamed across Europe, carrying their own huge, two-handed swords and waded into massed rows of enemy infantry, cutting and hacking a passage through for the cavalry.

Long, fluted grip

Spearpointed blade

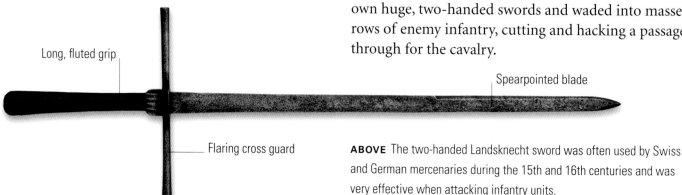

Flaring cross guard

ABOVE The two-handed Landsknecht sword was often used by Swiss and German mercenaries during the 15th and 16th centuries and was very effective when attacking infantry units.

During the 16th and 17th centuries, more accurate firearms and artillery were developed, and swords were relegated to a secondary role, although they were still regarded as the preferred weapon during close combat with the enemy.

17th- to 20th-century world swords

The introduction of the smallsword in the late 17th century highlighted the new requirement for both practicality and fashion. On the battlefield, the seasoned soldier knew that a more robust broadsword would always be required, such as the distinctive broadsword of the Scottish Highlander. Wide-bladed and double-edged, this broadsword had an enclosed basket hilt and was devastating when used at close quarters.

During the late 18th and early 19th centuries Europe and the outside world were rocked by countless wars and momentous battles. The swords carried by the major nations at war, particularly the French and British, are studied, as are the swords that were carried during one of the bloodiest conflicts outside Europe, the American Civil War.

However, by 1914, the sword had become obsolete in battle and, after the First World War, it was relegated to a purely ceremonial role. Indeed, during the rise of Nazi Germany the sword was worn as an accessory.

ABOVE The Battle of San Romano in 1432. The medieval battlefield normally comprised a mass of polearms and poleaxes which were used to inflict injuries both from horseback and on foot.

ABOVE A 19th-century Japanese print depicting a Samurai warrior with his sword. Their swords were often given names as a mark of devotion and a belief that their warrior spirit was contained within them.

Swords from Africa and the East

In Japan, the rise of the Samurai warrior class during the 12th century saw the development of the Samurai sword. These swords were forged in a complex and ritualized process. China also has a long history of sword making that stretches back over 3,000 years.

The Indian sword was almost totally unaffected by the influences of the West. Even when the British Empire had established virtually complete control over this vast country, Indian swordsmiths continued to produce unique indigenous swords of superb artistry and quality, including the "talwar" and the "khanda". In Africa, there was a dramatic division in sword styles between the Muslim-influenced north of the continent, and the central and southern areas.

By detailing the history of the sword this book tells the story of empires, dynastys and world wars, but it also gives fascinating detail of the smaller world of individuals; the people who forged, carried, fought with, and often died by, the sword.

ABOVE This British Army officer's sword, c.1870, was not used in fighting but carried as a dress sword and only worn on dress occasions. It was a regimental sword of the Border Regiment, based in the north of England.

Dragon incorporated into handle

Design of the sword

Over the centuries, the sword has evolved into many different forms and style, but there is general agreement concerning how its parts should be named. From the hilt pommel to the blade fullers, sword makers have defined both types and parts of the sword in a way that makes it easier for us to understand this most universal of weapons.

Types of swords

Light cavalry officer's sword

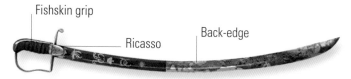

Fishskin grip

Ricasso

Back-edge

The curved blade of this cavalry sword was designed to provide the mounted horseman with an effective slashing and cutting weapon.

Rapier

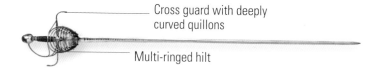

Cross guard with deeply curved quillons

Multi-ringed hilt

Rapiers are defined by their long, needle-like blades and complex, multi-bar hilts. They were purely thrusting swords and most effective when used in the duel.

Basket-hilted broadsword

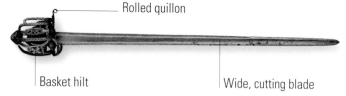

Rolled quillon

Basket hilt

Wide, cutting blade

The large, enclosed basket hilt protected the swordsman's hand, and the wide, double-edged, slashing blade was devastating at close quarters.

Smallsword

Grip

Pas-d'âne

The smallsword developed from the earlier rapier and usually took the form of a trefoil or three-sided blade. This blade shape provided exceptional strength.

Parts of a sword

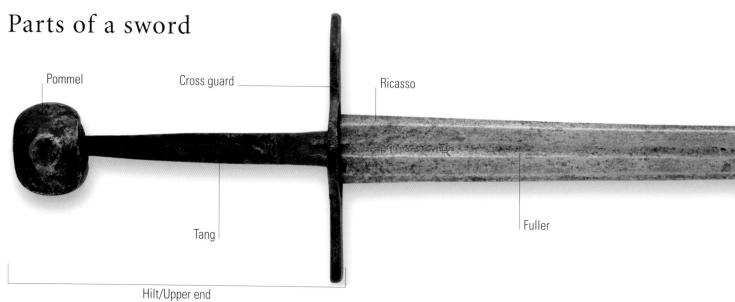

Pommel

Cross guard

Ricasso

Tang

Fuller

Hilt/Upper end

Types of blades

The sheer range of blade types that have been produced throughout history and across vast geographical areas is testament to the variety of functions that a sword could perform. Within any army or cultural group, different blades performed specific tasks. For example, cavalry swords were required to be of considerable length to enable the trooper to reach down and attack foot-soldiers. Blades were either curved or straight, depending on whether a thrusting or slashing motion was desired.

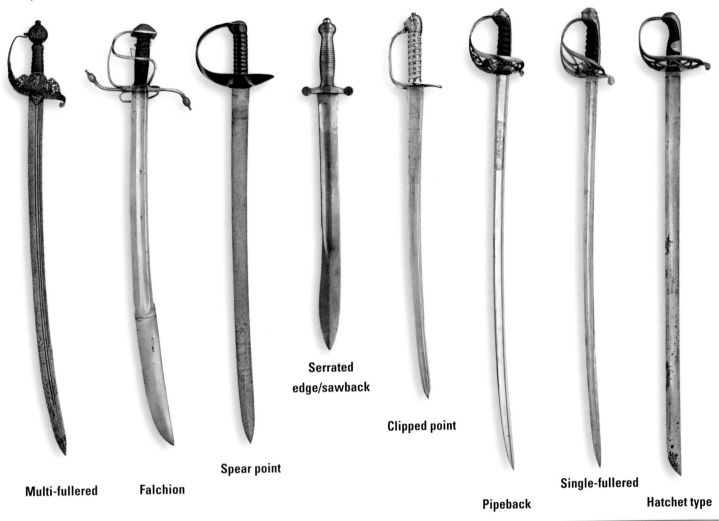

Multi-fullered

Falchion

Spear point

Serrated edge/sawback

Clipped point

Pipeback

Single-fullered

Hatchet type

A sword is a bladed hand weapon comprising a blade and a handle. The blade is usually manufactured in metal, with at least one sharp edge and a pointed tip for thrusting. The handle, called the hilt, can be made of many materials, but the material most commonly used is wood covered by leather, fishskin or metal wiring. A cross guard prevents the user's hand from slipping on to the blade.

Blade

Cutting edge

Blade tip

The origins of edged weapons

Around 2.5 million years ago, the first recognized edged tools were developed when so-called "Stone Age" peoples began to fashion simple hunting tools from flint and obsidian. The impact of prolonged droughts and the constant territorial battle for a reliable source of food inevitably led to conflict between neighbouring tribes. The weapons of hunting, including the axe and spear, were soon readily transformed into weapons of combat.

LEFT The Neolithic period is known as the New Stone Age. This ancient cave painting depicts a hunting scene in Libya.

antler horn. Finely crafted examples of these laurel-leaf points were unearthed in the 1860s at the prehistoric site of La Solutré, near Mâcon in Burgundy. Sources of good flint were highly prized; it is thought that some communities would travel up to 160km (100 miles) in order to obtain suitable working materials for tools and weapons. Such advanced tools were first used by Neanderthal man, and then *Homo sapiens*, around 35,000BC. *Homo sapiens* and later sub-groups (such as

Early use of tools

The first widespread use of tools occurred during the Palaeolithic Age (the Old Stone Age), between *c.*2.5 million and 8500BC. The hand axe was the most important tool of this period and would have been designed to provide both a cutting edge and a sharp point. It is impossible to assign to these axes a purely combative role as their primary function would have been either to attack animals or to remove their flesh and hide, but the axes would no doubt have been effective as both slashing and thrusting weapons. Flint and stone were shaped and tied to a wooden handle, and then bound with animal sinew and tendons. Later, in the Neolithic period (the New Stone Age), 13,000–8500BC, an opening was developed in the axehead to accept a handle.

The Stone Age spear was one of the earliest weapons used for hunting animals. Like the hand axe, the spearhead would have been secured by tying it with sinew or leather strips to a longer handle.

Hand-held flint and stone tools were gradually replaced by finely sharpened flint blades. The process of manufacturing such blades involved a technique known as pressure flaking, which involved skilfully knapping the flint with a pointed piece of hard wood or

---

The Clovis Spear point

Clovis flint points are the oldest known flint projectile points found in North America. They date to around 13,500 years ago and were used by the ancient peoples of the Americas, the Paleo-Indians. The first Clovis flint point was excavated in Clovis, New Mexico, in 1931. Many points were excavated alongside the remains of hunted Ice Age animals, particularly mammoths. The points are thin, fluted in shape and created from pressure flaking. Due to their small size, they were easily carried and became one of the first highly mobile edged tools, or possibly weapons, in human history. Inhabitants of the Americas in the Archaic period (8000–1000BC) are believed to be direct descendants of Paleo-Indians.

ABOVE This is an Archaic period Clovis spear point from the Americas. The Archaic period preceded the adoption of farming.

Cro-Magnon man) began to create semi-permanent agricultural settlements in the Old World between 35,000BC and 10,000BC.

From hunting to farming (7000–6000BC)

Following the end of the Ice Age (10,000BC), humans began to make the transition from semi-nomadic hunters to creators of established farming communities. The practice of agriculture began in the then fertile plains of Mesopotamia (comprising present-day Iraq, Turkey, Syria and Jordan). The natural requirement for defence of these settled areas also coincided with the development of more robust, edged weapons. One of the earliest excavated farming settlements can be found in the village of Çatal Hüyük (c.6700–5650BC) in central Anatolia (present-day Turkey). Numerous pressure-flaked projectile points and simple flint daggers were found during excavations, and indicate that the use of tools, whether for domestic or defensive purposes, had become an important part of daily life.

The Americas (8000BC–AD1000)

Paleo-Indians are believed to be the first people to have inhabited a large number of areas in the Americas about 11,000 years ago. It is thought that they were nomadic hunter-gatherers. Paleo-Indians are understood to have hunted with both fluted, stone-pointed wooden spears and the atlatl (a leveraged weapon that fired short spears). In addition, they probably foraged for edible plants. The Archaic period (8000–1000BC) is characterized by subsistence economies supported through the exploitation of nuts, seeds and shellfish. Between 1000BC and AD1000 Woodland Indians hunted small game and foraged in the forests.

The atlatl – Stone Age machine gun

Archaeologists believe that during the Palaeolithic Age, points or darts were attached to short wooden shafts and then mounted into sockets on heavier spear shafts. This created a form of reloadable, hand-held spear, or *atlatl* (taken from the Aztec language, Nahuatl).

The back end of the spear was fitted into the atlatl. The thrower would hold the atlatl and its flint dart in place, with the elbow bent and the hand resting beside the ear. A forward motion with the shoulder straightened the elbow and the wrist flicked the atlatl forward, creating the necessary momentum to propel the dart at great speed – an action which has been compared to that of a fly fisherman casting his line. Atlatl weights, commonly called "banner stones", are wide and flat shaped, with a large hole drilled into the centre. This may have been a clever improvement to the design as it made the atlatl quieter when swung, so it was less likely to alert prey or other hunters. However, another theory suggests that the banner stone was carried primarily by hunters as a spindle weight to produce string from natural fibres gathered while hunting.

Atlatls are thought to have originated in North Africa over 25,000 years ago. These weapons have been recreated in modern times and shown to have the potential to kill animals at 40m (131ft). Despite their obvious capability to kill humans, they are more likely to have been used for hunting and bringing down big game. Great skill would have been required to wield such a weapon although its accuracy tends to decrease when used over larger distances.

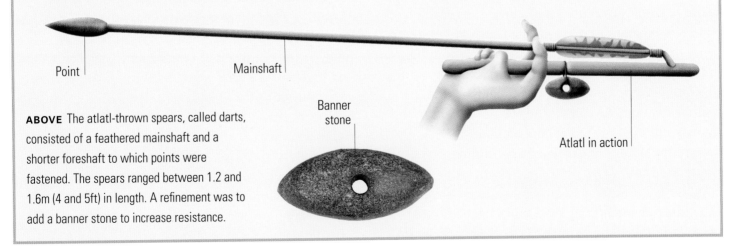

Point | Mainshaft

Banner stone

Atlatl in action

ABOVE The atlatl-thrown spears, called darts, consisted of a feathered mainshaft and a shorter foreshaft to which points were fastened. The spears ranged between 1.2 and 1.6m (4 and 5ft) in length. A refinement was to add a banner stone to increase resistance.

Bronze Age weapons

New technologies to refine, smelt and cast metal ores were first used during the Bronze Age (*c.*3500–700BC). Early civilizations in the Middle East began to combine bronze or copper alloys to produce spears, daggers, swords and axes. Later, swordsmiths started producing finely detailed swords with stronger iron blades. These techniques spread to China, India, South-east Asia and Europe, where they would have a profound influence on future warfare.

Pommel | Hilt | Raised strengthening ridge

Early metal weapons

With the introduction of copper alloys (90 per cent copper and 10 per cent tin), the bronzesmith was able to produce a much harder metal. Its hardness and consequent durability were wholly dependent on the temperature that could be achieved during smelting. The higher the temperature, the harder the metal would become. Iron ore was also discovered and soon became the material of choice for the production of bladed weapons. Iron ore was abundant and, like copper alloys, it could be heated to high temperatures by using charcoal. Immersion of the blade in water and continuous hammering to form a well-tempered blade developed a consistent surface that was less prone to fracture and breakage than bronze or copper. Most blades would have been cast in stone, metal or clay moulds.

The sword in Europe from *c.*2000BC

Although it is difficult to date precisely when the sword was first introduced into Europe, there is general agreement that long-bladed swords were being manufactured around 2000BC. Their appearance in Europe was probably independent of earlier developments in metalworking seen in the Near East and the Aegean. Distinctive flint swords have been found from this date in Denmark and northern Europe, including riveted bronze swords with triangular blades from the early Bronze Age.

In the later Bronze Age, swords were cast in one piece, including the grip and pommel (the knob at the top of the handle or hilt). Many differing pommel

ABOVE This short sword was made between 3200 and 1150BC. The decorated hilt and round pommel were later replacements.

shapes also emerged. One of the most common swords is the antenna (or voluted) sword. This had a two-pronged or scrolled, inwardly curving pommel, said to represent the outstretched hands of a human figure. Sword shapes also varied, from broad-leaf shapes to straight forms that featured grooves, sometimes erroneously described as "blood channels", but more likely to have been designed to provide a lighter and more easily wielded sword.

The carp's tongue sword

Common in western and eastern Europe around 1000BC were a group of bronze swords known as "carp's tongue" swords. A significant number of this distinct sword type were discovered at excavations in the Thames Valley and Kent during the mid-20th century. The most notable find was at the Isleham Hoard, in Cambridgeshire, England. It comprised more than 6,500 objects made of bronze, including many swords of carp's tongue design. They had wide, tapering blades which were useful for slashing, with a thinner, elongated end suitable for stabbing. This style of sword is thought to have originated in north-western France.

The socketed axe

Another important military innovation of the Bronze Age Mesopotamian armies in the Middle East, and one that would have an enormous impact on future

Hilt and blade cast in one piece

Leaf-shaped blade

BELOW These Bronze Age socketed axes were used as both domestic tools and close-quarter combat weapons.

ABOVE A complete Bronze Age sword (top) with hilt and leaf-shaped blade (*c*.1100BC) and a large bronze spearhead (bottom) from 700BC.

battlefield warfare, was the introduction of the socketed axe. Previously, ancient axe makers had struggled to keep the axehead firmly attached to the haft (the handle), especially when handling the axe with considerable force. The Sumerians devised a cast bronze socket that slipped over the haft and was secured with rivets. Its development was probably a consequence of the introduction of primitive forms of body armour and the need to penetrate this armour with sufficient force. Later axes would have narrower points that could be used to penetrate bronze plate armour. The axe would remain an integral battle weapon for the next 2,000 years.

The sickle sword of Mesopotamia

One of the earliest societies in which organized warfare was waged was the Sumerian culture of southern Mesopotamia (*c*.3000BC). Even at this early stage of human civilization, professional standing armies were being used to defend communities. Although the most common weapons used by the Sumerians, and later the Assyrians (*c*.1100–600BC), included the spear and bow, warriors also carried a sharply curved sickle sword.

Introduced around 2500BC, this all-metal sword had a single-handed grip and a blade of around three grip lengths. A stunning example in the British Museum,

London, England, has the following inscription on the blade: *Palace of Adad-nirari, king of the universe, son of Arik-den-ili, king of Assyria, son of Enlil-nirari, king of Assyria.* It is believed that this sword was owned by the Assyrian king Adad-nirari I, who conquered northern Mesopotamia (*c*.1307–1275BC). Mesopotamian art frequently depicts the sickle sword as a symbol of authority, and it is often seen placed in the hands of gods and kings.

BELOW An illustration of a sickle sword, 1307–1275BC, from the Middle Assyrian period (the reign of Adad-nirari I).

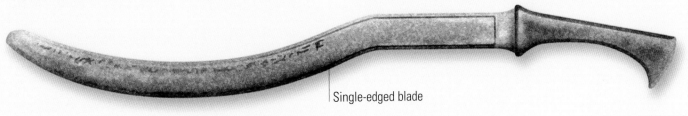

Single-edged blade

Ancient Egyptian weapons

The Egyptian armies of the Old Kingdom (*c.*2649–2134BC) and Middle Kingdom (*c.*2040–1640BC) fought primarily on foot and in massed ranks. Their soldiers were lightly equipped with shield, bow, spear and axe. The constant wars and invasions of the later dynasties brought with them the assimilation and transference of diverse military technologies. This greatly expanded their range of weapons, which diversified to include plate armour, chariots and, more importantly, the sword.

Introduction of the sword

Following the collapse of central government in Egypt due to internal rebellion, the Hyksos peoples of Palestine took advantage of this instability and invaded Egypt around 1640BC. They ruled Egypt for over 200 years and brought with them striking advances in weapon making, particularly the use of metal in the manufacture of swords and edged weapons.

The adoption of the sword in ancient Egypt was a direct consequence of the introduction of metal. Prior to this, axes and spears were fashioned from flint, and swords were simply not available. Copper had already been utilized for some time, but bronze was the first material consistently used for sword blades, as it was much harder and easier to work. Sickle-shaped swords (originally inherited from the Sumerians) were gradually replaced by swords with slightly curving blades. The "Sea Peoples", invaders from the Aegean and Asia Minor who first attacked Egypt during the reign of Merenptah (1213–1202BC), also introduced straight, two-edged blades with sharp, stabbing points. Contemporary depictions of battles show massed infantry using both jabbing and slashing swords.

The influence of iron

Throughout the Mediterranean during the New Kingdom period of Rameses III (*c.*1186–1155BC), the smelting of iron ore had a direct impact on Egypt, enabling swords to be produced with much longer and sturdier blades. Examples of swords with blade lengths of up to 75cm (30in) have been unearthed from royal tombs.

RIGHT This ancient Egyptian warrior is depicted carrying a long, double-edged and broad-bladed sword. It is probably a one-piece construction.

The spear

Primarily a weapon used for hunting, the Egyptian spear never surpassed the bow and arrow, which remained the standard weapon of the Egyptian Army. During the Old Kingdom (*c.*2649–2134BC) and Middle Kingdom (*c.*2040–1640BC), simple pointed spearheads were constructed from either flint or copper and attached to long wooden shafts by means of a tang (the hidden portion or "tongue" of a blade running through the handle). In the later New Kingdom (*c.*1550–1070BC), stronger bronze blades were secured by a more reliable socket.

Spears were made for either throwing or thrusting, and were especially useful when chasing fleeing enemies and stabbing opponents in the back. They were regarded primarily as auxiliary weapons and called upon by charioteers when they had spent all their arrows and needed some form of close protection. The following description of Amenhotep II's victory at the Battle of Shemesh-Edom *c.*1448BC (in Upper Galilee, now modern-day

LEFT Carved by an unknown Egyptian artist during the 18th Dynasty, *c.*1567–1320BC, this relief depicts two soldiers, one carrying a spear.

The khepesh – sword of the Pharaoh

Originally a throwing weapon of sickle-sword shape, the khepesh could also be used as a conventional slashing or cutting sword. It appears to have been a favoured weapon of the Pharaoh, as he is often depicted wielding it against enemies or during a hunt. The discovery of the tomb of Tutankhamun (r.c.1361–1352BC) by Howard Carter in 1922 revealed remarkable insights into the lives of ancient Egyptians. One of the numerous objects found in the tomb included a ceremonial shield, which depicted the young Pharaoh "smiting a lion" with a khepesh.

Inside edge

ABOVE The Tomb of Tutankhamun. The king is depicted in a number of battle scenes, although it is not known whether he actually took part in any campaigns.

Ivory handle

ABOVE An Egyptian bronze khepesh sword with a handle inlaid with ivory. The sword comes from El-Rabata and dates to the New Kingdom, c.1250BC.

Israel) is recorded at the Temple of Karnak (built over a period of some 1,600 years from around 1500BC), near Luxor in Egypt:

Behold His Majesty was armed with his weapons and His Majesty fought like Set in his hour. They gave way when His Majesty looked at one of them, and they fled. His Majesty took all their goods himself, with his spear…

Karnak Stele of Amenhotep II
from W.M. Flanders Petrie, *A History of Egypt, Part Two.*

The battle-axe

There were two distinct types of battle-axe used by the Egyptian soldier: the cutting axe and the piercing axe. The cutting axe, used during the early kingdoms, had a head attached to a long handle and would have been used at arm's length. The blade head was attached to the handle through a groove and then tightly bound with leather or sinew. This axe was especially effective against opponents who wore little body armour, particularly Egypt's African enemies, like the Nubians. It was usually deployed after the enemy had been routed (often by the archers), rather than as a weapon against massed ranks.

The cutting axe was later superseded by the piercing axe that was designed to penetrate armour. Unlike contemporary Asiatic societies (especially the Sumerians and the Assyrians), who used a blade cast with a hole through which the handle was inserted and firmly attached by rivets, the Egyptians continued to use the antiquated method of a mortise-and-tenon joint (a tenon is a tongue that slots into a hole called the mortise) to fix the blade to the handle. This made the battle-axe inherently weaker. During the invasion by the Hyksos around 1640BC, this obsolete weaponry, coupled with the invaders' use of horse-drawn chariots, long swords and stronger bows, proved fatal for the lightly armed Egyptians.

ABOVE A painted relief of light infantry with standards, battle-axes and palm fronds, from the temple of Hatshepsut in Thebes, Egypt, c.1480BC.

Ancient Greek weapons

The ancient Greeks (*c.*750–146BC) regarded the sword as strictly an auxiliary weapon, one that would never supplant their battle-proven reliance on the spear. The spear enabled the heavily armoured hoplites, or infantrymen, to stand together and protect each other within the close formation of their phalanx wall of shields and spears. This allowed them to repeatedly fight and win battles against far superior opposition.

The hoplites

Infantry foot-soldiers, the ancient Greek hoplites (from the Greek word *hoplon*, or armour) formed the military backbone of the Greek city states. Hoplites were recruited mainly from the wealthier and fitter middle classes, and bore the financial responsibility to arm themselves. Bronze armour, sword, spear and shield all had to be provided from solely private means. Hoplites were not full-time professional soldiers whose only life was war. They had volunteered to serve their state only in times of war (usually in the summer), and, if they survived, would return afterwards to their civilian roles. The hoplite was a true manifestation of the classical Greek ideal of shared civic responsibility.

ABOVE Mosaic showing Alexander the Great, leader of the Macedonians, hunting a lion with a doru (spear) in the 3rd century BC.

The spear

A Greek infantryman's main battle weapon was the spear, or doru. Measuring around 2.7m (8.8ft) in length, it would have been held in one hand, while the shield (aspis) was grasped in the other. The spearhead was leaf-shaped, socketed and made of iron. At the butt of the shaft was a sharp bronze spike, or sauroter ("lizard killer"), which could be thrust into the ground for added stability. In extremis, when the spearhead was broken, the sharp spike could be flipped around and used as a weapon of last resort.

The Macedonians, under the leadership of Alexander the Great (356–323BC), also developed their own spear or pike, the sarissa. Little is known about it, but it is thought to have been up to twice the length (around 4–5m/13–16.4ft) of the doru and had to be wielded underarm with two hands. This meant that the usual protection of the shield-and-spear phalanx could not be utilized, and so a small shield, or pelte, was strapped to the left forearm. The sarissa's great length meant that it could keep the opposing troops at a distance, enabling the Macedonian cavalry to wheel around the flanks of an enemy and strike with devastating effect.

ABOVE Spartan hoplites, *c.*500BC, wearing Corinthian helmets. In addition to the shield and spear, hoplites would have also carried a sword.

The phalanx – ancient armoured fist

Derived from the Greek word *phalangos* (meaning "finger"), the hoplite phalanx was made up of a tight formation of spearmen, armed with large, concave shields that rested on the soldier's left shoulder and protected the man next to him, thus forming an all-enveloping, locked curtain of defence. The phalanx

was typically about eight men deep, with the front ranks projecting their spears forwards. The key to the success of the phalanx was the ability of the soldiers to keep together and not break the formation. This was not always easy, especially for the first few ranks, who were the main combatants, as the rear ranks' main purpose was to continually push their phalanx forward and maintain its shape.

There has been much debate as to how the spear was used while in the phalanx: was it held aloft or under the arm? Some authorities believe that it had to be held aloft, as it would have been impractical for a hoplite to hold his spear underarm, in case the sharp butt spike injured the man behind him. The use of the sword by the hoplites in the phalanx would have been regarded as a highly dangerous manoeuvre, because it necessitated breaking up the shape and, consequently, the defensive cohesion of the phalanx.

LEFT A stone depiction of Greek hoplites standing in phalanx formation, from *c*.400BC.

The sword

There is great irony in noting that the most successful sword design of the Ancient World was developed by the Greeks, who were ostensibly spearmen. The sword was never regarded as a main battle weapon and played a purely secondary role. Once the spears had been thrown or lost in battle, swords were then engaged to finish the conflict in a decisive manner.

The main battle sword of the ancient Greek military was the xiphos. Introduced around 800–400BC, it comprised a straight, double-edged, leaf-shaped blade of around 65cm (25.6in), and was particularly effective at slashing and stabbing. The Spartans carried a slightly shorter sword of the same design as the xiphos. This design probably influenced the later Roman gladius, or short sword.

Mounted Greek cavalry used a curved sword, or makhaira (meaning "to fight"). It had a large, slightly curved falchion-type blade and was designed to deliver a heavy slashing blow at speed.

The use of a curved blade for mounted horsemen would remain a constant feature of cavalry swords for the next 2,500 years.

ABOVE A frieze from the Mausoleum of Halicarnassus, *c*.350BC, depicting a mythical battle between the Greeks and the Amazons.

Ancient Celtic weapons

The warrior Celts (*c.*600BC–AD50) were famed for their ferociousness and tenacity in battle, and even received grudging respect from their Roman adversaries. The early Celts fought mainly on foot (later in chariots and on horseback), and relied heavily on the awesome psychological and physical impact of a massed charge of their warriors. Armed with either sword or spear and protected with little more than a shield or helmet, they defeated the mighty Roman legions and, in 390BC, even sacked Rome itself.

Symbolism of the Celtic sword

The Celtic sword symbolized to its owner power, strength, honour and ultimate glory in battle. The fine quality and extraordinary skills required to produce these swords meant that they were extremely expensive and normally reserved for nobles and chieftains. The sword was often buried with its owner amongst his many other possessions, or symbolically thrown into water as a gift to the gods or spirits.

The falcata

With a large inwardly curving, single-edged blade rather like a kukri (heavy, curved Nepalese knife), the falcata was an extremely devastating weapon. Hilts were iron, hook-shaped and sometimes decorated with stylized horse or bird-head pommels. The origin of the falcata was pre-Roman and it is likely to have been a development of the ancient Greek sickle-shaped sword, or kopis. The sword could deliver a very powerful blow, something akin to an axe strike but with the slashing capabilities of a conventional sword. Contemporary Roman writers often describe how the falcata had the capacity to split both shield and helmet. The Celts of Hispania (Spain) were said to be the most feared exponents of this sword and it was a common weapon encountered by Roman forces during the early years of the Roman Republic (509–124BC).

The manufacture of the falcata

During this possibly unique process of manufacture, various forged steel plates were buried in the ground, usually for more than three years, and allowed to corrode. They would then be dug up and any weak or spurious metal would be separated and discarded. Any remaining good steel was reforged again through the traditional Celtic method of pattern welding – the practice of forming a blade from several metal pieces of differing composition. The blades were then forge-welded together and manipulated to form a pattern, making it considerably harder. In response to these much tougher blades, the Roman legions redesigned their shields and armour to give them more protection. The introduction of the Roman gladius, or short sword, was said to be a direct reaction to the Roman soldiers' battlefield experience of the falcata.

Longer Celtic swords

The growing use of cavalry and, later, the war chariot meant that Celtic warriors needed a longer sword to effectively reach down and strike at an opponent.

LEFT Relief plaque, made from copper with silver and gold plating, of a warrior wielding a long-bladed Celtic sword from the 1st century AD.

These long swords, with an average blade length of around 70cm (27.5in), had wood, bone or horn hilts, with blades manufactured in iron or steel. Scabbards were normally constructed from plates of iron and suspended from a belt of iron links.

The Celts were one of the first European peoples to discover how to smelt iron, and by the time they made contact with the Romans they had developed consistent methods of producing better balanced swords that were more resilient and longer. It is therefore curious that the Roman writer Polybius (c.203–120BC) reported that, at the Battle of Telamon (225BC), the Gauls had carried inferior iron swords which bent at the first stroke and had to be straightened with the foot against the ground. This is also mentioned by Plutarch (c. AD46–127), but it seems more likely that this was Roman propaganda, as subsequent archaeological testing of excavated Celtic sword blades indicates that the quality of the iron and steel was quite exceptional.

The spear

A standard battlefield weapon for the Celtic warrior, the Celtic spear or javelin normally comprised an ash wood pole around 2m (6.5ft) in length, fitted with a large iron, leaf-shaped and socketed spearhead.

ABOVE Three Celtic spearheads from the La Tène period, each with a leaf-shaped, finely ridged, slightly bent blade. Two of the examples have holes in the socket for attaching the head to the shaft.

Following military experience gained after initial contact with the Roman armies from the 1st century AD, the Celts changed the design of their spearheads so that they possessed a narrower profile. This was a reaction to the Roman use of protective body armour and the need to find a spear that could effectively puncture their plate. Spears and javelins were also carried in bunches by young warriors, or "gaesatae". These were paid mercenaries who had gained a fearsome reputation for their bravery. Once they had thrown all the spears at the enemy, they would retrieve them from the ground or their opponents' bodies.

The swords of the La Tène culture

Archaeological finds from the La Tène settlement on the north edge of Lake Neuchâtel in Switzerland, dating to around 500–1BC, highlight the Celtic genius for creating swords with complex abstract and organic decoration on both the hilt and the scabbard. Blades were double-edged and straight, and made from pattern-welded iron or steel. They are found in both long and short versions. Many finely worked hilts also feature human heads and other anthropomorphic and zoomorphic motifs.

RIGHT A 1st or 2nd century BC sword and scabbard from La Tène in Switzerland.

Ancient Roman weapons

The army of ancient Rome (800BC–AD476) was a formidable fighting force – well disciplined, organized and supplied with an array of effective and battle-proven weapons. The sword and spear were the infantryman's main weapons, and the spectacular military successes of the Roman legions throughout Europe and the Near East lay in the disciplined battlefield application and relentless training in the use of these weapons.

The gladius

A short stabbing weapon with a blade length of around 50–60cm (19.6–23.6in), the gladius was the primary fighting sword of the Roman soldier. Its origins are somewhat uncertain, simply because very few examples have been unearthed by archaeologists and the only identifiable gladii have come not from Italy but from Germany. This sword was described by the ancient Romans as the "gladius hispaniensis", in recognition of a similar type of Celtic design encountered by the Romans during their conquest of Hispania (modern-day Spain) during the Second Punic War (218–201BC). Before this, Roman soldiers would have used swords of Greek origin.

The hilt, or capulus, of the gladius featured a rounded grip, moulded with four finger ridges to allow a comfortable and firm hold upon the sword. Pommels were bulbous and normally of plain form. The scabbard was made of wood, covered with leather and strengthened by a rigid frame of brass or iron.

Wearing the gladius

Although in later centuries most swords would be worn traditionally on the left side, the gladius was worn on the right side. This allowed the wearer to draw with the right hand and at the same time carry a heavy shield in the left hand. This can be confirmed from the depictions of Roman soldiers on tombstones, wall paintings and friezes. The tombstone of Annaius Daverzius, an auxiliary infantryman who served with the Cohors III Delmatarum, a Roman garrison stationed in Britain during the 1st century AD, shows his sword attached on the right side of his belt by four suspension rings. As an acknowledgement of his status, a centurion was allowed to wear his sword on the left.

RIGHT Legionaries, carrying gladius swords, are depicted during battle in a relief carving from the base of a column found at Magonza, Italy.

The gladius in battle

If used with enough force and directed at the most vulnerable parts of the body, particularly the stomach, the stab of a gladius blade into the flesh of an opponent was nearly always fatal.

Roman soldiers fought as a single fighting unit within an organized and massed formation. This fighting block comprised hundreds of men standing

ABOVE A battle between Roman and Germanic armies, depicted as a relief on a marble sarcophagus, *c.* AD180–190.

shoulder to shoulder. They had to keep this formation solid and it was crucial, therefore, that all soldiers fought with the gladius placed in their right hand. Any left-handed recruit would have this hand strapped behind his back during training, and it would be kept tied until he learned to fight with the right hand as well as he would have done with the left. Wearing the gladius on the right also meant that the drawing of the sword would not interfere with soldiers on either side, and would also not restrict the use of the Roman scutum (the shield).

The Roman line would wait for the enemy to come right up to it and then await the order to advance. Upon receiving this order, all soldiers would take one step forward and thrust their shields, or scuta, into the bodies and faces of the enemy, causing them to lose their balance and so render them temporarily vulnerable. The shield was then quickly withdrawn and the gladius thrust into the body of the opponent. The Roman soldier was taught to deploy the gladius horizontally, so piercing the enemy's ribs and penetrating to his vital organs.

BELOW A gladius and scabbard, which belonged to an officer of Tiberius (42BC–AD37), the second Emperor of Rome.

Etched gold decoration

Traces of wood from scabbard

Steel blade, badly rusted and corroded

ABOVE A stone depiction of the Emperor Hostilianus in a Roman battle scene, 251AD. He is carrying a gladius, of which the blade is broken.

The spatha

By the middle of the 1st century AD, the gladius had been replaced by the spatha (*spada* is the modern-day Italian word for sword). It had a much longer blade (60–80 cm/23.6–31.5in) and shorter point. The sword was Celtic in origin and it is probable that Gallic cavalry (from Gaul, in modern-day France), in the employ of Rome, introduced the sword to the Roman Army during the time of Julius Caesar (100–44BC) and Augustus (63BC–AD14). It was a slashing weapon and designed to be used by both the Roman cavalry and infantry.

ABOVE Found in Spain, this is the only known actual example of a spatha with an eagle-headed hilt. It would have been used by a tribune in the early 4th century AD.

The manufacture of swords

By the time of the Roman Republic (c.509–44BC), the use of steel in the manufacture of swords was well advanced and Roman swordsmiths smelted iron ore and carbon in a bloomery furnace (the predecessor of the blast furnace). The temperatures in these furnaces could not achieve the high levels required to fully melt the iron ore, so the swordsmith had to work with pieces of slag (residue left after smelting) or bloom (mass consisting mostly of iron), which were then forged into the required blade shape. These pieces or strips of cooling metal were welded together for increased blade strength. During this process the owner's initials or full name were sometimes engraved onto the blade.

The pilum

Around 2m (6.5ft) in length, the main heavy spear or javelin used by the Roman Army was the pilum. It consisted of a socketed iron shank with a triangular head. The pilum weighed in at around 3–4kg (6.6–8.8lb); later versions produced during the Empire (27BC–AD476) were lighter. The pilum would have been thrown by charging legionaries and could easily penetrate shield and armour from a range of around 15m (49.2ft). A lighter, thrusting spear, the hasta, was also used for close-combat situations.

The narrow, spiked shape of the spearhead meant that when it became stuck in the wood of an opponent's shield it was extremely difficult to dislodge, so disrupting the opponent at a critical moment of battle. He might have to relinquish his shield, leaving himself extremely vulnerable to the oncoming Roman infantry. Even if he was able to remove the spear, he couldn't throw it back at the Romans because the soft iron of the spear shank meant that it bent on impact and so became useless as a weapon. In the aftermath of a Roman victory, used pila were gathered from the battlefield and sent back to the Roman Army blacksmiths for straightening. The Roman military strategist Vegetius (c. AD450) comments on the effectiveness of the pilum:

As to the missile weapons of the infantry, they were javelins headed with a triangular sharp iron, eleven inches or a foot long, and were called piles. When once fixed in the shield it was impossible to draw them out, and when thrown with force and skill, they penetrated the cuirass without difficulty.

from *De Re Militari* (c. AD430)

Later, a further development of the pilum was introduced: the spiculum. Vegetius notes its power:

They had likewise two other javelins, the largest of which was composed of a staff five feet and a half long and a triangular head of iron nine inches long. This was formerly called the pilum, but now it is known by the name of spiculum. The soldiers were particularly exercised in the use of this weapon, because when thrown with force and skill it often penetrated the shields of the foot and the cuirasses of the horse.

from *De Re Militari* (*c.* AD430)

The contos

A long, wooden cavalry lance which was 4–5m (13.1–16.4ft) in length, the contos derived its name from the Greek word *kontos*, or "oar", which probably gives some indication as to the length of the lance. It took two hands to wield, so the horseman had to grip his mount by the knees. To be able to do this effectively would have taken considerable strength and training.

ABOVE Made in the Roman provincial style, this contos lance head dates from the 2nd century AD.

LEFT Roman soldiers carrying light spears (lancea) and shields. Detail of a relief from the Antonine Column, Rome, erected *c.* AD180–196 in recognition of the Roman victory in battle over a Germanic tribe.

BELOW Dating from AD70, this inscribed Roman commemorative stone depicts a horseman (Vonatorix) wielding a spear.

Saxon weapons

Around AD400, the Saxons came to England with a reputation for warlike ferocity and a strong reverence for the sword as a potent symbol of both strength and martial spirit. The mass of Anglo-Saxon warriors normally carried a shield and dagger (seax) and fought with spears and axes. More sophisticated members of the nobility and professional soldiers carried spears (similar to the Roman pilum) and swords.

The Saxon sword

Through excavating numerous graves in England, archaeologists have learnt that the Anglo-Saxons often chose to bury their dead with a full array of weapons and armour. These grave weapons are normally of great beauty and artistry, highlighting the belief that a warrior needed to take with him into the afterlife (or in later Christianized Anglo-Saxon society – heaven), material proof of the great status afforded to its owner while alive.

Ownership of both sword and spear defined the Anglo-Saxon warrior as a free man, compared with slaves (oeows) who were forbidden from carrying any arms. The great cost of acquiring a serviceable sword would also have shown the owner to be a man of means and rank. A typical Anglo-Saxon sword had a long, straight, double-edged blade with an average length of around 90cm (35.4in).

The Saxon spear

In Anglo-Saxon burial grounds, the spear is by far the most common type of weapon unearthed and is regarded as the primary armament of the Anglo-Saxon warrior. All ranks of society carried the spear, from king and eorl (earl), to the lowly ceorl (free man of the

Double wings

Long spearhead for deeper penetration

ABOVE A winged Saxon spearhead (top) with double wings to prevent an opponent's blade travelling down the spear. A slim spearhead (bottom) to allow penetration through armour.

lowest rank) or conscripted peasant. Comprising a leaf-shaped iron spearhead and wooden shaft, traditionally made of ash, a typical spear measured around 1.5–2.5m (4.9–8.2ft) in length.

The spear would have been held in one hand while a shield was grasped in the other. It was extremely effective when used in a mass formation, most notably the famous Anglo-Saxon "shieldwall" or shildburh. It was this shildburh that faced William the Conqueror at the Battle of Hastings. It was only compromised when

BELOW In a detail from the Bayeux Tapestry, 1082, the English soldiers, who are all on foot, protect themselves with a shield wall while the Normans mount a cavalry attack.

The Saxon battle-axe

Anglo-Saxon warriors inherited the two-handed "bearded" battle-axe from earlier generations of Danish Viking invaders who had employed it with great effect to board enemy ships. The Anglo-Saxons soon became extremely proficient at using the battle-axe. With its 1.2m (3.9ft) haft and large honed axehead of around 30cm (11.8in), it had the capacity to shatter shields and inflict grievous wounds. Swung from side to side, it could cut down a mounted soldier and his horse in a single blow.

These long axes were wielded by the huscarls (King Harold's personal bodyguards) and described as cleaving "both man and horse in two". One of the drawbacks of using the two-handed axe is that while raised above the head it momentarily left the user dangerously exposed at the front to sword or lance thrusts. Despite this, the sight of a mass of axe-wielding Anglo-Saxon warriors approaching the enemy's ranks normally had the desired psychological effect, with many contemporary accounts noting that the opposition simply fled from the battlefield.

RIGHT A later depiction of the felling of King Harold II (c.1022–1066) by a Norman arrow at the Battle of Hastings (1066).

the Normans feigned a cavalry retreat, deliberately allowing themselves to be chased, whereupon they suddenly wheeled back and charged the openly exposed Anglo-Saxons. This was a fatal error by the pursuers and dictated the eventual outcome of the battle.

In contemporary descriptions of the Battle of Maldon in AD991 (situated on the modern-day Essex coast in England), the Anglo-Saxon Eorl Byrhtnoth is depicted as throwing two types of spear or javelin, both long and short. It is interesting that it was only when injured by a Viking spear, and finally exhausting his supplies of spears, that he eventually resorts to using his sword.

Anglo-Saxon women warriors

It was not only men who fought and became respected heroes during the Anglo-Saxon period. Recent archaeological discoveries have raised the possibility that women also took part in warfare.

In the village of Heslerton, in North Yorkshire, England, two female burials were unearthed in 2000. Dated to around AD450–650, both women had been buried with spears and knives. Just outside Lincoln, a town in eastern England, the skeleton of another Anglo-Saxon woman warrior (c. AD500) was found with a dagger and shield.

Procopius (c. AD500–565), the late Roman Byzantine scholar, notes in his history of the Gothic Wars (AD535–552) that an unnamed Anglo-Saxon princess, from the tribe of Angilori and described as "the Island Girl", led an invasion of Jutland (western Denmark) and captured the German King Radigis of the Varni.

Aethelflaed, eldest daughter of Alfred the Great of England (c. AD849–899), was known as the Lady of Mercia and was at the forefront of many battles against the invading Vikings. Aethelflaed was also responsible for the construction of a number of Anglo-Saxon fortifications.

The Sutton Hoo sword

The sword is part of a magnificent hoard of royal Anglo-Saxon treasures found in a huge ship grave, in Suffolk, England, in 1939; its design is based on the earlier Roman spatha, or cavalry sword. Its decoration includes a hilt comprising a beautiful gold and cloisonné garnet pommel and gold cross guard. The iron blade is heavily corroded but the original pattern welding is still identifiable and includes eight bundles of thin iron rods hammered together to form the pattern. This would have given the sword exceptional strength, although it is more likely that it was produced solely as a sumptuous grave gift.

Viking weapons

The Vikings were Scandinavians who colonized parts of Europe from the 9th to the 11th century. Vikings revered the sword above all weapons. The passing of a family sword from father to son was considered a major event. Even better was the knowledge that a sword had been wielded in battle or in a feud by a great warrior or nobleman. This gave the sword added status and was thought to imbue the blade with special powers. The Viking armoury also included the spear and battle-axe, the first-line weapons launched against an enemy.

Double-edged blade

Viking weapons

The main Viking battlefield weapons employed during first contact with the enemy were the spear and battle-axe. One of the reasons why the sword usually took a secondary role in the initial phase of a battle was that the continual striking of one sword edge against another would have inflicted large nicks to the blade and eventually removed the consistency and effectiveness of its finely sharpened edge.

Because of this, once the spear or axe had done its work, the Viking warrior would then draw his sword and look for exposed and softer areas of the body to attack. Skeletons of Viking battlefield victims unearthed by archaeologists consistently exhibit more spear wounds than sword cuts, highlighting the selective use of Viking swords in battle.

The Viking spear

A Viking warrior's most common battlefield weapon, the spear, comprised a simple iron, broad-leafed or spiked point on a wooden (normally ash) shaft, with a total length of around 1–2m (3.2–6.5ft). Spearheads with wings were called barbed spears. The spear was extremely effective and used for both thrusting and throwing, with larger-headed spears being used for cutting. There is evidence that the spears used to cut through chainmail were used one-handed as well as two-handed. A skilled Viking spearman was reputed to be able to throw two spears at once, using both hands, and also to catch a spear in flight and hurl it back at the opposition. A sword was then used in close-combat fighting.

LEFT A 9th-century Viking-decorated stone carving from Gotland, Sweden, depicts two soldiers fighting with swords.

Pommels and scabbards

The Viking sword pommel (located at the end of the hilt) is one of the most distinctive characteristics of a Viking sword. Most pommels were cast in solid iron (its weight providing a counterbalance to the weight of the blade), but there are also fine examples in bronze and also of iron inlaid with sheets of silver. Pommels ranged from the early pyramidal shapes of c. AD800 to the later, more complex pommels that were formed from triangular segments.

The great artistry and imagination of the Viking metalworker is clearly evident in these pommels and cross guards, with complex interlaced and geometric patterns worked in both silver and bronze gilt.

A scabbard (sheath or case) was made of two carved pieces of wood, glued at the sides and sometimes covered in leather or fur. The mouth and chape (the metal plate at the point) of the scabbard

ABOVE A Viking sword hilt with a cocked hat or lobed pommel. The decoration includes stamped abstract cartouches.

were sometimes mounted with decorated silver or bronze gilt. The sword would have been carried using a baldric (waist or shoulder belt).

The Viking battle-axe

When wielded with appropriate force, the Danish long-handled or "bearded" battle-axe was a devastating weapon. Its design was based on domestic Viking wood-splitting axes found throughout Scandinavia during the Viking period and evolved for use in battle. The battle-axe had a much larger head of either crescent or convex shape, which favoured downward blows, with a long wooden haft measuring 1–2m (3.2–6.5ft) in length. Sometimes blades were forged with an especially hardened double edge. They could also be forged quite thinly to give the user a lighter, more easily handled weapon.

The Viking sword

About 70–80cm (27.5–31.5in) long, the wide, double-edged blade of a Viking sword had shallow fullers, or so-called "blood grooves". The grooves were not actually designed to allow the blood to run down easily but rather to reduce the weight of the blade and give it added flexibility. The Vikings had a very close relationship with their swords, borne out by the personalized names they gave them, including Gramr ("Fierce"), Fotbitr ("Leg-biter") and Meofainn ("Decorated down the middle"). Swords were not common or inexpensive weapons and it is likely that they were mainly carried by persons of rank and wealth.

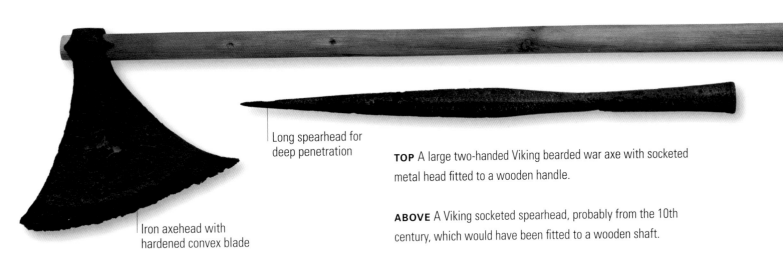

Long spearhead for deep penetration

Iron axehead with hardened convex blade

TOP A large two-handed Viking bearded war axe with socketed metal head fitted to a wooden handle.

ABOVE A Viking socketed spearhead, probably from the 10th century, which would have been fitted to a wooden shaft.

Viking sword manufacture

The smelting of iron ore with carbon to produce fine steel was well known to the Vikings and contributed to their reputation for producing blades of superb quality. They are best known for the complex process of pattern welding employed in their manufacture.

Modern X-ray technology of surviving blades now enables us to see how Viking smiths produced patterned blades by welding long strips of iron and steel together, forging them into square rods then finally twisting or folding these rods into small bunches, so creating the hard inner core of the blade. The outer cutting edge of the blade was welded to this inner core, using the best steel. Finally, the blade was carefully ground and polished with acid to reveal the extensive patterning.

Smiths worked hard to produce their own distinctive patterns. Their pride in such skilled work resulted in many blades being engraved with their makers' names, notably "Ulbehrt", "Lunvelit" and "Ingelri".

RIGHT A 12th-century carving from a wood panel in a church in Setesdal, Norway, depicts a scene from the Norse legend of Sigurd (Siegfried). Here, the dwarf Regin and his helper are shown forging a sword on an anvil.

Viking sword duels

The Vikings engaged in formal duels, or holmganga, to settle feuds. Holmganga roughly translates as "island going" and indicates that most duels took place on small islands where limitations of space (and, consequently, options for retreat), could be strictly enforced. The area of combat was determined by the laying out of a square cloth. Furrows were marked out around the cloth and the space was enclosed by a rope. Each of the combatants was allowed a second whose role was to hold the warrior's shield. Swords were the weapon of choice.

The duel did not commence with both warriors rushing at each other. Instead, each man took his turn at making one strike against his opponent. If a combatant chose this opportunity to back off and in so doing placed his foot outside the cloth, he was deemed to have run away and the fight would be stopped. If a strike was effective and incapacitating, the wounded party was allowed to stop the fight but was then obliged to forfeit a sum of money to his winning opponent.

RIGHT Two swords that display the distinctive punched and geometric decoration that was common on Viking sword pommels.

Orkneyinga Saga

Settling a feud by single combat with swords is a common theme in Viking sagas. One of the most famous accounts of the bloody use of a sword in such a feud is retold in the *Orkneyinga Saga* (*c.*1200), a unique historical narrative of the Orkney Islands that covers the period from its capture by Norwegians in the 9th century until the early 1200s.

The saga recounts how Rognvald, a Norwegian chieftain who ruled Orkney in *c.* AD860, was burnt to death in his own home by two of Harald Fairhair's sons. Bent on revenge, Rognvald's son Einar struck down and killed one of Harald Fairhair's sons, Halfdan Halegga. The victim's body was found the next day on the side of a hill, and the shape of an eagle had been cut into his back with a sword. More gruesomely, the ribs had been removed from the backbone and his lungs splayed out to represent the eagle's wings. Einar believed this display a worthy sacrifice to the Norse war god, Odin.

RIGHT The Norse god Odin with his sword and two ravens. He was the god of war and battle and the bringer of victory.

The sword in Viking sagas

The Vikings were great storytellers and believed that recounting tales was a gift, handed to them by the all-powerful war god, Odin. Without any means of writing them down, the Viking storytellers or skalds prided themselves on recalling epic stories and passing them on to others. Through these tales, the Vikings ensured that details of their religious beliefs and adventures were passed on from one generation to the next. Skalds were often employed by kings who wanted to be revered throughout their kingdoms. Although the stories were likely to have been exaggerated by the skalds, there is probably some truth in their telling of the events that occurred.

The ancient sagas of both the Vikings and the Anglo-Saxons frequently refer to the great strength of a sword blade and its apparent capability to hew a man in two. Sword strokes were aimed primarily at the head and neck, and were calculated to be killing blows. The following description from a later Icelandic text, describing events in the 10th and 11th centuries, underlines the devastating effect of a single sword blow:

Then Thorbjorn rushed upon Grettir and struck at him, but he parried it with the buckler in his left hand and struck with his sword a blow which severed Thorbjorn's shield in two and went into his head, reaching the brain.

from *Grettir's Saga* (*c.*1400)

ABOVE A detail from a stone carving from Gotland representing Valhalla, the great hall of the god Odin. Here warriors enjoyed a glorious afterlife awaiting the final battle against the forces of evil.

Medieval weapons

Feudal armies in Europe from the 11th to the 14th century produced a core group of premium fighting men – the mounted knights. Over time, they became more heavily armoured and reliant upon the shattering force of horse, lance and wide-bladed sword. In their wake, massed ranks of foot-soldiers engaged the enemy with long polearms (essentially weapons mounted on the end of a long pole), hoping to dismount and finish off any enemy knight. The fighting was brutal and bloody, conducted in a crush of jabbing, thrusting weapons.

1066 – the battlefield

The Battle of Hastings (1066) saw William of Normandy (*c.*1028–1087) unleash the devastating power of his heavily armoured knights for the first time on British soil. During many hours of hard fighting, King Harold II (*c.*1022–1066) and his fellow Anglo-Saxon defenders were constantly harried by repeated Norman cavalry charges. This type of mounted and mobile warfare was unknown to the Anglo-Saxons, who were predominantly foot soldiers, and it was only their fortunate selection of superior and defensible terrain prior to the battle that stopped them from being immediately overwhelmed.

The Norman war sword

A double-edged, razor-sharp broadsword with an average length of around 75cm (29.5in), was the main battle weapon of the Norman knight of the medieval period. It was ideal for swinging at speed and downward slashing. It would be used one-handed and in conjunction with a large, kite-shaped shield.

LEFT In this detail from the Bayeux Tapestry, Harold II's Anglo-Saxon troops, led by an armoured standard bearer and a warrior with an axe, confront a Norman cavalryman armed with a lance.

BELOW This sword is a "transitional" piece between the Viking and medieval period. It has a distinctive "brazil nut" pommel that was common in the early medieval period and the cross guard has increased considerably in width, while the blade is also more finely tapered.

Straight, squared cross guard

Fuller (bevelled groove) extends to almost complete length of tapered blade

LEFT A 13th-century French soldier. He carries a double-edged broadsword with brazil nut pommel and down-sloping cross guard.

BELOW RIGHT William the Conqueror, accompanied by knights and soldiers, from a page of illustrated Latin text from the 14th century.

The Norman lance

Although it is called a lance, Norman knights used what could more accurately be described as a long, wooden spear with a simple, spiked end. It would be held firmly under the arm in order that the maximum force of both man and horse could be transmitted into the charge. Once the enemy had been engaged, the lance could also be transformed into an effective close-combat thrusting weapon, or simply thrown.

The "knightly" or "arming" sword

During a period when there was a practical need for a substantial and sturdy fighting weapon on the battlefield, the medieval "knightly" or "arming" sword was carried. Most battles in Europe took the form of two heavily armed and armoured scrums locked in a frenetic life-or-death struggle to push the enemy back, coupled with the added difficulty of trying to kill or maim as many enemies as possible in a very limited amount of space. It was quite common for soldiers to be literally crushed to death by their own side as the battle moved along.

Sword manufacture

Before the 9th century good sources of quality iron ore were not always available and many swords were often forge-welded from a selection of smaller iron pieces, thus reducing the inherent strength of the blade. Conversely, swordsmiths also forged high-quality swords using a process known as pattern welding, using rods of superior iron. The process required that the rods be tightly twisted together, so creating a much stronger and more durable blade with great qualities of tempering. The interlocking of these rods under great heat, and their sudden cooling and hammering, created distinctive forging patterns on the blade's surface. This diversity of swirling patterns was highly prized by an owner.

By the 9th century in Europe, the blast furnace became widespread and the need for pattern welding diminished. During the centuries that followed, the technique was slowly lost, and by 1300 there are few examples of its use. The technique survived, however, in Scandinavia, where good-quality iron ores and charcoal were widely available.

ABOVE The knights Galahad and Gawain are pictured taking part in a tournament, from *La Queste el Saint Graal*, c.1316. The knights wield wide-bladed, slashing swords typical of this period.

Swords would have been pattern forged or "braided" in the manner of earlier Viking swords, making them excellent fighting weapons – very strong and not prone to breakage. Swords were normally combined with either a large shield or buckler (small shield), although there are many contemporary images and written descriptions that describe the use of the knightly sword without a shield. This was thought to enable the free hand to grab or grapple with opponents. A knight would have worn this large sword whether in armour or not. He would have been considered "undressed" without his sword.

The typical style of the "knightly" or "arming" sword was firmly established by the 12th and 13th centuries. In general terms, it comprised a long, broad-bladed cutting and thrusting sword with double fullers (bevelled grooves); a plain crossbar hilt; and a wheel, brazil nut, ovoid or mushroom-shaped pommel. This sword design had remained virtually unchanged since the Viking invasions (AD793–c.1066), and over the next three centuries there was to be little innovation. Most blades and hilts were plain, although some surviving blades are found with inlaid decoration, mostly in the form of large, punched lettering or symbols, normally of a religious or mystical nature. Pommels of this period can also be found with inset heraldic devices, denoting particular royal or noble families. Rare specimens have pommels of agate, inlaid gold or rock crystal.

Medieval ceremonial swords

Swords produced specifically for use at royal coronations and similar ceremonies began to appear from the 11th century onwards. They were not designed for battle and were kept safely in churches, palaces and state arsenals. Decoration was profuse and the scale was deliberately large and impressive. One of the swords of Charlemagne (or Charles the Great), King of the Franks (r. AD742–814), is preserved in the Schatzkammer (Treasury) in Vienna. The blade is single-edged, slightly curved and overlaid with copper decoration, including dragon motifs. Hilt and scabbard are covered in silver gilt. The grip is wrapped in fishskin, set at an angle and very reminiscent of Near Eastern swords of the period. The second sword sometimes attributed to Charlemagne is found in the Louvre, Paris. The ornamentation on the hilt suggests it was carried by him, but it was also known to have been used as a ceremonial sword when Philip the Bold was crowned in 1270.

RIGHT A line drawing of one of two swords attributed to Charlemagne or Charles the Great (r. AD742–814). The sword is kept in the Louvre Museum in Paris.

Large, rounded pommel with flattened sides

Cruciform-shaped cross guard

Blade graduating to spear point

LEFT A knight's sword, c.1250–1300, with a narrow blade, light enough to use on foot. This sword has a spear-point blade and impressive cutting and thrusting capabilities.

Downward-curving quillons

Blade with strong needlepoint for penetration

ABOVE A longsword with a highly tapered blade which could be used to penetrate armour.

The medieval sword in battle

A contemporary Florentine description of the Battle of Kosovo, between the Serbs and the Ottoman Empire in 1389, highlights the "knightly" aspect of the use of the sword and its perceived retributory power.

Fortunate, most fortunate are those hands of the twelve loyal lords who, having opened their way with the sword and having penetrated the enemy lines and the circle of chained camels, heroically reached the tent of Amurat himself…Fortunate above all is that one who so forcefully killed such a strong vojvoda by stabbing him with a sword in the throat and belly. And blessed are all those who gave their lives and blood through the glorious manner of martyrdom…

Response from the Florentine Senate (1389)

The medieval longsword

A natural progression from the two-handed "arming" or "knightly" swords of the early to mid-medieval period was the first longswords, with the main difference being an increase in blade length. The double-edged blade was 80–95cm (31–37in) long and weighed in at approximately 1–2kg (2.2–4.4lb). This was very much a sword of the late medieval period and was used from around 1350 to 1550. The length of the grip was also extended to allow a more powerful and directed use of two hands, but the traditional cruciform hilt was still retained.

The longsword was a new departure in sword design and this innovation was soon witnessed in its battlefield application. It had the usual cutting

ABOVE A 14th-century French battle scene. The chaotic nature of a medieval battle is very evident.

functions expected of a broadsword but the blade profile had become thinner and was now designed (through stiffening of the blade tip) to thrust and penetrate plate armour. The longsword would come to prominence during the Renaissance, when the battlefield became a testing ground for new forms of penetrative edged weapons. The terms "hand-and-a-half sword", "greatsword" and "bastard sword" are different classifications of swords of this period.

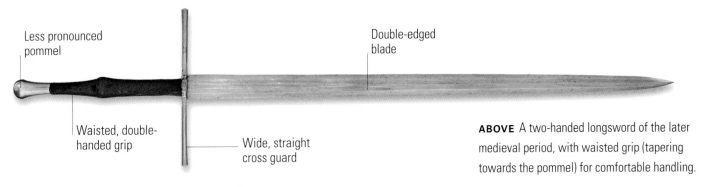

Less pronounced pommel

Double-edged blade

Waisted, double-handed grip

Wide, straight cross guard

ABOVE A two-handed longsword of the later medieval period, with waisted grip (tapering towards the pommel) for comfortable handling.

Medieval polearms

Massed formations of infantry soldiers carrying polearms was a common sight on the battlefields of Europe from the medieval period right through to the early 1700s. The fighting part of the polearm was placed on the end of a long shaft and they were specially designed to disable and inflict crushing injuries upon knights. Cheap to produce in large numbers and versatile on the battlefield, these weapons became the mainstay of the European medieval foot-soldier when engaged in close combat.

The bardiche

A particularly brutal polearm used extensively in medieval and Renaissance Europe, the bardiche found particular favour in eastern Europe and Russia. Blade design varied considerably from country to country, but the main characteristic was a substantial cleaver-type blade and attachment to the pole by means of two widely spaced sockets. Blade length was around 60cm (23.6in), although the haft was unusually short at approximately 1.5m (4.9ft). This weapon appeared top-heavy and impractical, but the bardiche was regarded more as a heavy axe and wielded accordingly.

The bill

With a tradition going back to the Viking Age, the bill is commonly regarded as the national weapon of the English both during and beyond the medieval period, although it was used elsewhere in Europe, particularly Italy. As with many polearms, the bill developed from an agricultural tool, the billhook, and displayed a hooked chopping blade with several protruding spikes, including a pronounced spike at the top of the haft, resembling a spearhead. The bill also had a strong hook for dismounting cavalry. Used skilfully, it could snag onto any loose clothing or armour and wrench

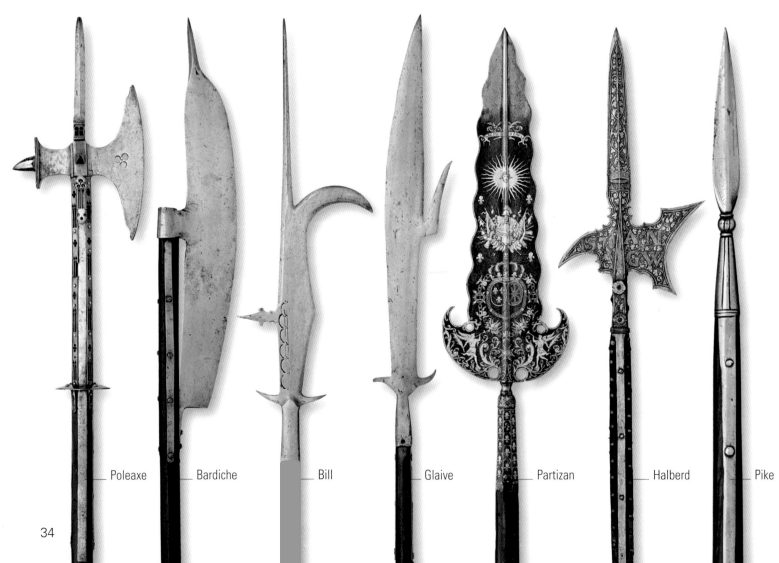

Poleaxe — Bardiche — Bill — Glaive — Partizan — Halberd — Pike

the target from his horse and throw him to the ground. English bills tended to be shorter with the emphasis more on the chopping action of the blade, while Italian bills had a very long spiked end, resulting in its use as a thrusting weapon.

The glaive

Similar in design to the Japanese naginata, the glaive originated in France, and its single-edged blade was attached to the haft by means of a socket shaft. Blade length was typically around 55cm (21.6in), with a wooden pole 1.8–2.1m (5.9–6.8ft) long. Medieval Swedish infantry adapted the glaive by fixing a double-edged sword blade to the haft. Glaives with small hooks are known as "glaive-guisarmes".

The halberd

The halberd is a crude, rectangular blade, shaped to a point at the top; the earliest known use of the halberd comes from an excavated example from the battlefield at Morgarten (1315) in Switzerland. The word "halberd" originated from the German halm (staff) and barte (axe). Over time, the halberd's spear point was improved to allow it to be used to repel oncoming horsemen. The haft of the halberd was also reinforced with thick metal rims, making it more effective and durable when blocking blows from an enemy sword or axe.

ABOVE The battle of Pavia, 1525, between the Holy Roman Emperor Charles V and Francis I of France. Note the pikes and halberds (right).

The partizan

Smaller than normal polearms at 1.8–2m (5.9–6.6ft), the partizan was constructed from a spearhead or lancehead, with an added double axehead at the bottom of the blade. It proved not to be as effective as other polearms and it was gradually withdrawn from frontline use. It remained as a ceremonial weapon and many have elaborately decorated blades. Partizans were carried right through to the Napoleonic Wars (1804–15).

The pike

A ubiquitous battlefield weapon during the medieval period, the pike was simply a very long, thrusting spear employed by infantry as both a static defensive weapon against cavalry attacks and as an attacking polearm, when used in massed ranks and close formation. The combined length of both haft and head rose over time to a staggering 3–4m (9.8–13.1ft), sometimes even 6m (19.6ft), and it was this very length that was both its strength and also its inherent weakness. The pikeman could stand at a relatively safe distance from close combat, but the weapon's unwieldiness could also prove dangerous for him. A pikeman was armed with sword, mace or dagger in case his pike was lost in battle.

Medieval and Renaissance jousts

Jousts and tournaments took the form of individual combat between armoured knights, mounted or on foot, using lances, swords, axes and maces. Jousting was first practised in the early Middle Ages. During these colourful public events, two knights fought to enhance their martial reputation. The melée, a tournament (or tourney), provided the audience with the spectacle of many knights involved in mass trials by combat. Compared with warfare proper, this form of organized "entertainment" was only one step away from the real thing.

Origins of the tournament

The first written record of a formulated set of tournament rules is usually credited to a Frenchman, Geoffroi de Purelli, in 1066. Unfortunately, his guidelines were of limited use to him as he was killed at the very tournament for which he had composed the rules. Despite this early setback, the popularity of jousting was firmly established in western Europe by the 13th century and it continued as a public sport well into the 1600s.

Military service in the medieval period

Medieval knights were obliged to provide military service to their king, lord or liege on a regular basis. Warfare during this period, although perhaps exciting to a young knight on his first campaign, was, for most of those involved, extremely unpleasant. Living conditions were usually poor and, if the knight was not killed or badly wounded in battle, the combination of disease or hunger would normally carry him away. But there could be an opportunity for redemption amidst this state of wretchedness. By showing valour and courage on the battlefield, he had the opportunity to establish a martial reputation with the consequent possibility of great financial and social rewards from his master, or even the king.

On the other hand, equivalent fame and fortune, combined with regular practice in the use of weapons, could also be gained in peacetime and without embarking on a long and possibly fatal campaign of war. This alternative avenue was to be found in the joust and tournament.

RIGHT A knight is unhorsed with a jousting lance. The illustration is taken from the *Codex Manesse* by Walther von Klingen, Zurich, *c.*1310–40.

The individual joust

A joust was a horseback encounter between two knights with lances. The object was to unhorse the opponent. If a combatant struck either rider or horse with his lance, he was automatically disqualified. This was known as "tilting". If the opponent was not unhorsed but a clean hit was made to the centre or "boss" of his shield, points would be awarded.

LEFT A knight with jousting lance, *c.*1500. His plate armour includes an extra protective layer near his vulnerable left side.

The melée or tourney

Taking the form of massed trials by arms in a public arena, the melée or tourney was a popular part of the tournament in the 12th and 13th centuries (jousting became popular later on). It was a savage and brutal fixture, with many lives lost and serious injuries sustained. Upon hearing the call to charge, rival knights rode or ran onto the tournament field and proceeded to unhorse or attack their designated opponents with a selection of weapons, including broadsword, war axe, club or mace.

In some competitions, the melée was more organized, with combat restricted to a series of three strokes per weapon: for example, three tilts of the lance or three strokes of the sword, and the same for both battle-axe and mace. To actually kill an opponent during a tournament was considered morally wrong, although the ferocity of the combat sometimes inevitably led to fatalities.

RIGHT In this French 14th-century illumination the knight Lancelot is depicted in single combat, watched by King Arthur and Guinevere.

The jousting lance

Jousting lances were made of solid oak and it would have required considerable strength, force and accuracy to unseat an opponent. It would certainly have taken a significant strike to shatter a lance. Knights practised their technique against a specially constructed target, or quintain, a life-sized re-creation of an opponent's lance, helmet and shield. In modern-day re-creations of the joust, a lightweight, wooden lance is used in order that it can break more easily and so lessen the impact on an opponent.

Two types of horses were used during the joust. Warmblood chargers were selected for their stamina and quickness in the charge, whereas heavy warhorses or coldblood destriers were chosen for their large bulk, which made them deliberately slower but able to pack a heavier punch upon contact. Horses were trained to canter at an ambling pace to give their riders stability and enable them to focus and aim better with their lances.

RIGHT A selection of jousting lances. At the end of each lance was a coronal (crown-shaped metal cap) consisting of three or more metal prongs, designed to catch onto the opponent's shield.

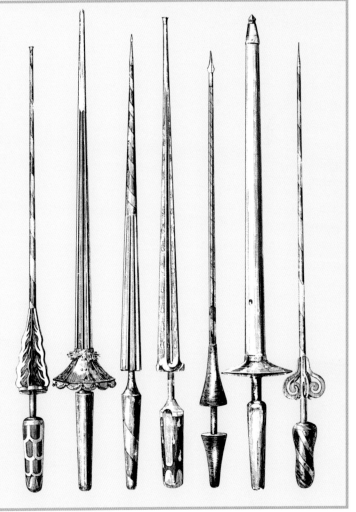

Swords of the Renaissance

The soldier of the mid-1500s witnessed dramatic advances in military technology. Swords, bows and pikes were now being challenged by early artillery, hand-held guns and complex siege weapons. In response, combatants became more heavily armoured. The sword evolved from being a purely slashing weapon to one that could pierce and break through plate armour. New sword types also appeared, from the huge two-handed broadsword of the Landsknecht to the handy short-bladed falchion of the ordinary infantryman.

ABOVE A Polish estoc, which would have been used by the cavalry. The needle-like blade was ideal for penetrating armour.

The estoc or tuck sword

Stiff, lozenge or diamond-shaped thrusting blades were now replacing the wide-bladed and cruciform-hilted swords typical of the medieval period. This new type of sword was known to the French as an estoc and to the English as a tuck.

The estoc featured a long, two-handed grip, enabling the bearer to achieve maximum effect as he thrust the sword downwards into armour. This sword was particularly effective at splitting chainmail and piercing gaps in armour. Due to the narrowness of the blade, it had no discernible cutting edge but a very strong point. Opponents who had lost the protection of their armour during the heat of battle were still dispatched by the traditional double-edged cutting sword, held in reserve for just such an eventuality. Versatility and a range of weapons to hand was still an important and practical factor.

The "hand-and-a-half" sword

Common throughout Europe from the beginning of the 15th century, the "hand-and-a-half sword" is also referred to as a "longsword". The contemporary term "bastard sword" derives from it being regarded as neither a one-handed nor a two-handed sword. Despite these perceived drawbacks, it possessed a reasonably long grip and shorter blade, which allowed one hand to hold the narrow grip firmly, while a couple of fingers placed strategically on the forte gave the soldier extra leverage and manoeuvrability when wielding. The length of these swords was around 115–145cm (45.3–57in).

The falchion

Although the falchion's design had originated in ancient Greece, the sword experienced a widespread revival during the Renaissance, particularly in Italy, France and Germany. This short-bladed sword had a straight or slightly curved blade, with cross guards either absent or very simple.

BELOW The "hand-and-a-half" sword has a short grip that accommodates one hand, while the fingers of the second hand are placed on the blade forte to allow extra leverage and control when swinging the blade.

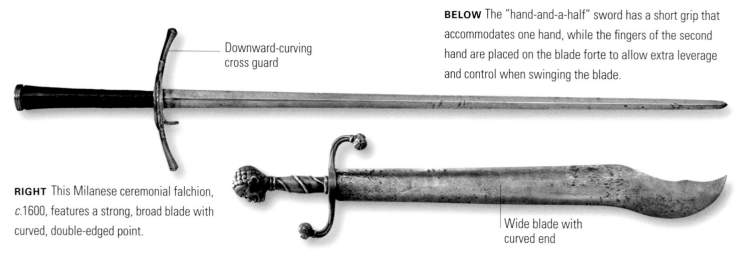

Downward-curving cross guard

RIGHT This Milanese ceremonial falchion, *c.*1600, features a strong, broad blade with curved, double-edged point.

Wide blade with curved end

Two-handed (Zweihänder) swords

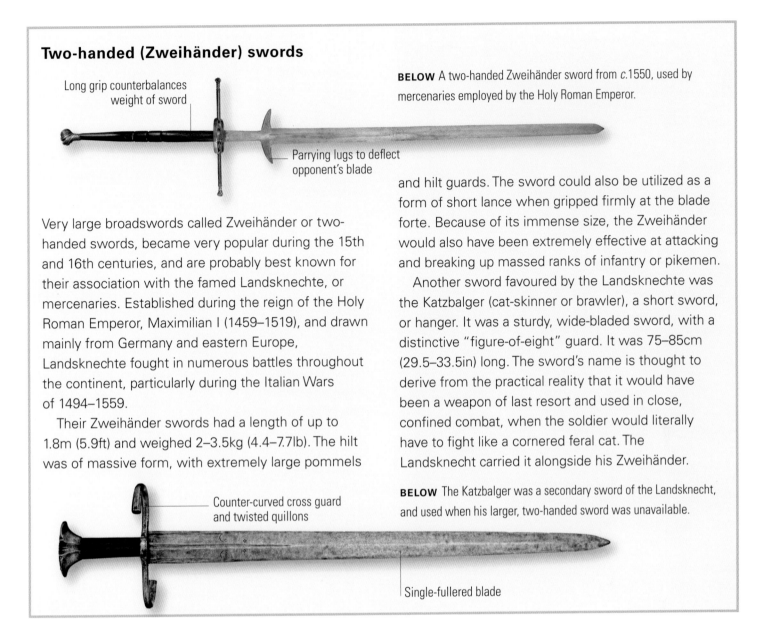

Long grip counterbalances weight of sword

BELOW A two-handed Zweihänder sword from *c.*1550, used by mercenaries employed by the Holy Roman Emperor.

Parrying lugs to deflect opponent's blade

Very large broadswords called Zweihänder or two-handed swords, became very popular during the 15th and 16th centuries, and are probably best known for their association with the famed Landsknechte, or mercenaries. Established during the reign of the Holy Roman Emperor, Maximilian I (1459–1519), and drawn mainly from Germany and eastern Europe, Landsknechte fought in numerous battles throughout the continent, particularly during the Italian Wars of 1494–1559.

Their Zweihänder swords had a length of up to 1.8m (5.9ft) and weighed 2–3.5kg (4.4–7.7lb). The hilt was of massive form, with extremely large pommels

and hilt guards. The sword could also be utilized as a form of short lance when gripped firmly at the blade forte. Because of its immense size, the Zweihänder would also have been extremely effective at attacking and breaking up massed ranks of infantry or pikemen.

Another sword favoured by the Landsknechte was the Katzbalger (cat-skinner or brawler), a short sword, or hanger. It was a sturdy, wide-bladed sword, with a distinctive "figure-of-eight" guard. It was 75–85cm (29.5–33.5in) long. The sword's name is thought to derive from the practical reality that it would have been a weapon of last resort and used in close, confined combat, when the soldier would literally have to fight like a cornered feral cat. The Landsknecht carried it alongside his Zweihänder.

BELOW The Katzbalger was a secondary sword of the Landsknecht, and used when his larger, two-handed sword was unavailable.

Counter-curved cross guard and twisted quillons

Single-fullered blade

The falchion was primarily a side-weapon and was usually carried by the infantry. Because of its short blade and ease of manoeuvrability, the falchion became the precursor to the hunting sword.

The cinquedea, or "five-fingered" sword

Another distinctive short sword that developed in Italy during the Renaissance was the cinquedea. The shape and form of the cinquedea typifies the Renaissance belief in the importance of artistry, combined with a newly rediscovered passion for the classical world. It was worn mainly with civilian dress and comprised a very wide blade of five-fingered

span. The hilt was normally of simple form, with a severely waisted grip. Because of its wide blade, many swordsmiths took the opportunity to embellish the swords with exquisite engraving and gilding. The sword would have been worn in the small of the back in order that it could be drawn laterally.

There is some debate as to whether the cinquedea was actually a dagger rather than a sword. The average length is noted at 40–50cm/16–19in (and there are even two-handed versions known), so this probably indicates that the cinquedea fits more comfortably within the broad family of swords rather than dagger types.

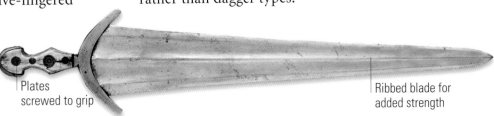

RIGHT A cinqueda sword, with typical pronounced medium ridge, or spine, running down the centre of the blade.

Plates screwed to grip

Ribbed blade for added strength

ABOVE Sword and scroll of Anne de Montmorency, 1493–1567, from the *Hours of Constable Anne de Montmorency*.

Ceremonial swords

The increasing power and wealth of the European monarchies and city states during the Renaissance meant that the sword did not only serve a purely military function. It also became a manifestation of the rank and status of the privileged, and its most notable appearances were at royal coronation ceremonies. Although the medieval cruciform-hilted sword had fallen out of favour on the Renaissance battlefield, being superseded by more complex and enclosed-hilt forms, it was still retained for ceremonial purposes – perhaps recalling a more "knightly" time – when a gentleman or courtier swore allegiance to his king by the kiss of a knightly sword. These "bearing" swords were carried before kings, queens and senior clergy. The sword of Frederick I of Saxony, presented to him by Emperor Sigismund I of Germany in 1425, has a cruciform hilt inset with rock crystal and heavily gilded in gold and silver. There is also a massive 15th-century bearing sword, supposedly made for either Henry V of England or Edward, Prince of Wales, which has a total length of over 228cm (88.6in). Ceremonial swords were also presented as symbols of state office. From the 14th century onwards, English mayors were granted the right (usually by the monarch) to carry a great civic sword on ceremonial occasions. This tradition was upheld for centuries and many historic towns in the United Kingdom still retain these swords. The earliest recorded civic sword still in existence is to be found in Bristol and is thought to date from around 1373. Constables of France, including such notables as Bertrand du Guesclin and Anne de Montmorency, carried bearing swords.

In terms of sheer brilliance of decoration and craftsmanship, the ceremonial swords presented by the Renaissance popes must rank as the apogee of 16th-century sword decoration. Given with a richly embroidered belt and cap by the pope each year on Christmas Day, invariably to members of the European Catholic nobility, these great two-handed swords were fabulously ornate and featured a profusion of precious stones and extensive gold and silver metalwork.

The development of hunting swords

Hunting had always been the favoured and exclusive pursuit of the nobility since the early medieval period and Renaissance hunters continued this pastime with vigour. The depiction of the royal hunt was a popular subject for artists and many painters and weavers of tapestry found the drama of the chase and final kill with sword and spear irresistible.

The falchion sword, or short hanger, was well known to the infantry as a side-weapon. It was first adopted during the 14th century, specifically as a dedicated hunting weapon. In later years, a saw-back blade was also incorporated for ease of cutting up the kill, followed by the development of a specialist set of tools for pairing. This combination of sword and skinning tools was known as a garniture, or trousse. As the owners of these hunting swords invariably had great financial means, decoration of the swords became ever more elaborate.

LEFT An illustration of a hunting sword with pommel and crossbar decorated by birds' heads. It has a saw-back blade for cutting the kill.

Swords of justice, swords of execution

Inscription

Great swords were also employed as both symbols and facilitators of judicial law. Many local courts of justice placed a large bearing or executioner's sword on the courtroom wall. The presence of the executioner's sword was not purely symbolic for it had a practical application in the actual beheading of prisoners. It was often highly decorated and engraved with prayers for the condemned, warnings against transgressions and vivid images of beheadings, hangings and torture.

Executioners' swords were more common in continental Europe from the 1400s, particularly Germany, with England still preferring the axe. The sword hilt was normally of conventional cruciform shape with a large counter-balancing pommel. It was very well constructed, with high-quality steel used for the manufacture of the blade. The blade edge was extremely sharp and it was a requirement of the executioner to keep it well honed so that the head of the victim could be severed in one mighty blow. Blades were broad and flat backed, with a rounded tip. The sword was designed for cutting rather than thrusting, so a pointed tip (as in the case of military blades) was unnecessary.

ABOVE This German executioner's sword has a double-edged blade with a blunt, lightly rounded point. Many surviving "execution swords" are actually swords of justice which would be carried before the judge to indicate his power over life and death.

ABOVE In this detail from the above sword, an etched inscription can be seen. In German it reads "*Ich Muß straffen daß verbrechen – Als wie Recht und Richter sprechen*". Translated, this means "I have to punish crime as the law and judge tell me".

An executioner's sword in the British Museum, London, has the following words engraved on the blade in Latin. It translates as: "When I raise this sword I wish the sinner eternal life / The Sires punish mischief: I execute their judgement." When no longer used for executions, swords became ceremonial.

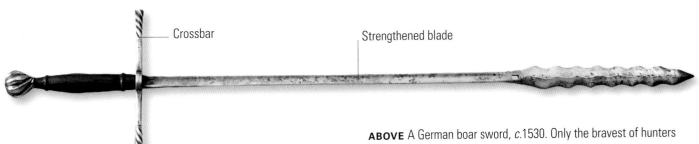

Crossbar

Strengthened blade

ABOVE A German boar sword, *c.*1530. Only the bravest of hunters used swords rather than spears for boar hunting.

Another sword designed solely for the hunt was the boar sword. Based on the triangular-bladed estoc or tuck, its greatly stiffened blade was designed to withstand the power of a charging boar or other large animal. The boar sword was introduced during the 14th century and by around 1500 it had developed a faceted or leaf-shaped spear point. A crossbar was later added near the end of the blade to prevent an animal running up the length of the blade and so making it difficult to retrieve.

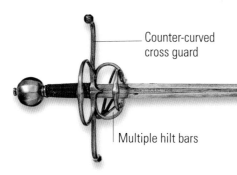

Counter-curved
cross guard

Multiple hilt bars

BELOW A German rapier dating from *c.*1560–70. It has a large spherical pommel that counterbalances the weight of the blade.

The rapier

Spain is normally cited as the first country to have introduced the rapier, or *espada ropera* (sword of the robe), during the late 1400s. This designation highlighted the new-found ability for a gentleman to wear these swords with ordinary civilian dress, rather than needing to don his armour. Italy, Germany and England adopted the rapier soon afterwards.

In its most complete and recognizable form, the rapier came into full prominence during the early 16th century. In the mid-1400s, precursors of the rapier (including the standard cruciform-hilted sword) had begun to develop a primitive knuckle guard and forefinger ring or loop. By 1500, a series of simple bars were joined to the knuckle guard to form a protective hilt. At this time, the blade was still a wide, cutting type, and it is only well into the 16th century that the

slender rapier blade was fully developed. This typically thin blade was deemed impractical for use during heavy combat on the battlefield so the rapier was viewed primarily as a "civilian" duelling sword. The new rapier hilt, however, was adopted by the military but with the retention of a wider, more traditional broadsword fighting blade.

The blade

Sword blades were manufactured in Toledo and Valencia (Spain), Solingen and Passau (Germany), and Milan and Brescia (Italy). They were sold as unhilted blades and then hilted locally at their eventual destinations throughout Europe. Some blades are marked by their maker, although many are plain. Notable bladesmiths' names include Piccinino, Caino, Sacchi and Ferrara from Italy, Johannes, Wundes and Tesche (Germany) and Hernandez (Spain). Respected names were often stamped on blades by lesser-known rivals to enhance the value of an inferior sword.

BELOW Italian rapier, *c.*1610. Of true swept-hilt form, it has deep chiselling to the knuckle guard.

BELOW A North European duelling rapier, *c.*1635, with a distinctive elongated and fluted pommel.

BELOW A Spanish cup-hilt rapier, *c.*1660. The cup and hilt are extensively pierced. It has very long, straight, slender quillons with finials to each end.

BELOW An English rapier with a finely chiselled cup hilt, *c.*1650. The blade is stamped "*Sahagum*".

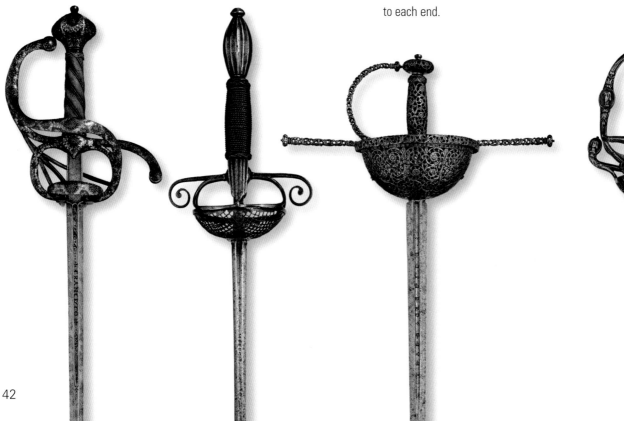

LEFT Two Italians fencing with broadswords. The rapier was later adopted as a cut-and-thrust civilian weapon used for self-defence and duelling rather than heavy combat.

The hilt

Renaissance swordsmen were presented with many differing styles of rapier, which had developed over time and in different areas. This difference was normally displayed in the sword hilt rather than the blade. To make identification clearer, historians have divided the hilt into a series of distinct evolutions from primary, basic, quarter, half, to three-quarter and then full hilts. Some examples have just a simple loop and knuckle guard, while later rapiers exhibit multiple ring guards and S-shaped upswept and downswept quillons (cross pieces at right angles to the blade and hilt). These later, more extravagant rapiers are commonly described as being of "swept-hilt" form. Large ovoid or octagonal pommels were necessary to counterbalance the weight of the long blade.

The development of the rapier

In the 16th century, the first 50 years could truly be called the age of the rapier. This century witnessed the rapier being worn as the ultimate fashion accessory and signifier of rank. Great competition was placed at Court to be the nobleman with the most grandly ornate sword, and contemporary paintings vividly show the wide range of rapiers available to those willing to pay the vast sums needed to purchase such a "trophy" piece.

By the end of the 16th century, blade lengths had reduced, making the rapier more manageable in the hand. Hilt design had now become significantly complex and, with increased blade-to-blade action, more emphasis was laid on protecting the hand. In the 1600s we see the addition of more side plates and shell guards for this purpose.

The rapier and fencing

Modern fencing emerged during the latter half of the 15th century and is directly attributable to the development of the rapier as a weapon of choice for a gentleman. The first fencing manuals were published in Spain in 1471 and 1474. In Germany, the Marxbruder and Federfechter fencing guilds were given a letter of privilege by Emperor Friedrich III in 1478, enabling them to recruit members and teach the art of fencing.

In Italy and central Europe a left-handed dagger (main gauche) was developed and used in conjunction with the rapier, and sometimes also a small shield, or "buckler", would be used to parry the sword blows. More noblemen died during the 16th century from duelling than conventional warfare.

RIGHT A sword fight with rapiers. This illustration was taken from a woodcut, *c.*1656.

17th- and 18th-century swords

A dramatic change in sword design appeared in the 17th and 18th centuries. The long-bladed rapier of the Renaissance and the great two-handed sword of the Landsknechte had become obsolete as the changing nature of war relegated the sword to a more secondary role, being steadily overtaken by more reliable and destructive firearms. Despite this, the military sword was still regarded as an effective weapon. Civilian gentlemen now carried smaller, lightweight, ornamented swords, as dictated by the changing fashion of the day.

ABOVE A French smallsword, from *c.*1770. The blade is decorated with scrolling foliage, highlighted in blue and gilt.

The smallsword

Towards the end of the 17th century, the need to carry a substantial sword in civilian life diminished and gentlemen began to adopt a sword of smaller proportions. It was described as a "town", "walking" or "court" sword and would later develop into the smallsword proper. In England, this change coincided

with a period of relative social stability after the English Civil War (1642–51), and a growing belief that there was less need to be heavily armed when going about one's business.

These early "transitional" or part-rapier smallswords were more practical when used in close order combat (particularly the now-popular duel), and were also considered more comfortable to wear alongside the civilian dress that had now superseded the wearing of armour in public.

The traditional rapier hilt was also replaced by new hilt styles from the 1700s, including a stylized shell guard and smaller quillons, thinner knuckle guards and a wider range of pommel styles. Extra *pas-d'âne* rings (the inwardly curving quillons that reached the base of the shell guard) were added to the hilt. *Pas d'âne* literally means "a donkey's steps".

LEFT In *Portrait of a Gentleman, c.*1640 (oil on canvas), the subject carries an early form of basket hilt, combined with a backsword blade.

BELOW An ornate French smallsword hilt, *c.*1760. The pommel, knuckle guard and shell guard are deeply embossed. The blade is engraved with numerous decorative motifs.

ABOVE Probably French with a Spanish blade. It is likely that this duelling rapier, *c.*1670, would have been used in conjunction with a gauntlet and cloak in the left hand, acting as a distraction to the opponent.

The function of the sword also changed. It had now become not just a weapon of defence or attack but also a distinctive signifier of rank and very much influenced by the vagaries of fashion. The smallswords worn at European courts were soon copied within society's more fashionable circles. During the late 17th and early 18th century, the dominant decorative influence in European society was French design and this became a powerful stimulus in smallsword design and decoration. The Rococo movement was at its height and the incorporation of shell-like curves, foliage and classical imagery is very evident in hilt design. Advances in technology and metalworking meant that smallswords were more easily manufactured in combinations of iron, steel, brass, silver and, occasionally, gold. The craftsmen who produced these smallswords were only limited by the depth of the client's purse and their own imagination. Consequently, the swords displayed a stunning range of quality, ornamentation and sheer creative elegance.

Military influence

As the 18th century progressed, the smallsword entered the military arena and was adopted by officers. Ordinarily, they tended to purchase more than one sword, and the smallsword, with its less robust, yet elegant proportions, was deemed more suitable for formal or "walking out" occasions, particularly parades and balls where it was seen as a status symbol. A more practical fighting sword of larger dimensions and wider blade was still carried into battle although some hilts were of smallsword design.

The colichemarde blade

In the late 1600s the normally flat rapier blade of the late Renaissance was superseded by an important technological breakthrough, when a group of German sword makers developed the colichemarde blade. This radical new blade shape was of trefoil, or three-sided, form and "hollow ground" with a hexagonal or diamond-shaped profile. The forte was also purposely wider and longer, giving the blade more strength. This new-found manoeuvrability allowed the weight of the sword to be concentrated in the hand, so providing more control and precision when thrusting.

The technical knowledge needed to produce these hollow-ground blades was jealously guarded by the German sword makers, despite attempts by the English government to bring over German workers. A rival sword factory was eventually established at Shotley Bridge in County Durham, in 1690. Its attempts at producing hollow-ground blades were not successful and it reverted to manufacturing swords of a more traditional and flat-backed design.

The popularity of colichemarde blades was quite short-lived and by the mid-1700s, blade shape was already changing again. The demise of the colichemarde blade was due partly to its greater suitability for duelling over everyday or military use.

RIGHT Duelling in the 17th century. The antagonist on the right has adopted a typical duelling pose.

LEFT A British dragoon officer, c.1795. He carries a curved stirrup-hilted sabre of the "hussar" type.

Cavalry swords

The cavalry sword was still a horseman's most effective weapon of defence and attack up to the 18th century. Unlike the infantry soldier, who began to rely more on musket and pistol, the cavalry soldier carried a firearm only as his secondary weapon of defence. It was therefore crucial that he had a sword capable of producing a devastating effect when combined with his horse's speed and his own strength and skill. The sword needed to be heavy and robust, with a long cut-and-thrust blade, fixed to a large hilt, affording good protection to the sword hand.

The use of a straight-bladed and single-edged cavalry "backsword" had been well established by the 1600s. These swords were carried throughout Europe and became the mainstay for cavalry formations. The early 18th century also witnessed the growing influence of cavalry sabres with curved blades. Their origins are

thought to be either Eurasian or Arabic. The Ottoman Turks had carried curved "mameluke" swords for many years. It is likely that the spread of the Ottoman Empire into eastern Europe by the late 1600s created an opportunity for western sword makers to examine captured examples of this new form of sword, eventually interpreting and converting them into more "western" sword styles.

Emergence of heavy and light cavalry

By the mid-1600s, European nations began to establish permanent standing armies, dividing them into designated infantry and cavalry regiments. Cavalry regiments took this transformation a stage further by making a distinction between light and heavy cavalry. The swords issued to these different branches of the army also changed, with the heavy cavalry carrying a long, straight, thrusting blade, and the light cavalry a slightly shorter, slashing, curved blade (although the widespread adoption of a curved blade would appear much later, in the early 1700s).

The backsword

Like most European nations, English cavalry troopers of the 17th century favoured a heavy backsword. Common hilt styles included an enclosed, multi-bar iron basket hilt with a large apple-shaped pommel. This design originated in Germany and northern Europe, and was later taken to a new level of sophistication by the work of Scottish basket hilt makers. The basket hilt, in many different forms, was carried by cavalry

BELOW A French cavalry backsword, dating from c.1690. The hilt is made up of a complex series of intertwined bars.

BOTTOM The blade of this English mortuary sword, c.1645, is double-edged and multi-fullered (a number of grooves).

Double-edged, narrow blade

Basket hilt

Pierced and chiselled guard

Thrusting blade

regiments well into the 18th century. Parallel to this was the development of a more robust "military" version of the newly adopted smallsword (normally for officers). It had a bilobate (two-branched) counter-guard, large ovoid pommel and broadsword blade.

The "mortuary sword" of the English Civil War

During the English Civil War (1642–51) the so-called "mortuary" sword was another peculiarly English sword type carried extensively. It was given the erroneous title "mortuary" by Victorian sword collectors because of the application of decorative work to the hilt that featured a series of engraved human faces, supposedly in memory of the beheaded Charles I (executed in 1649) and his wife, Henrietta Maria. Although there is a mortuary sword in the collection of HM The Queen at Windsor that bears a likeness to Charles I and his queen, mortuary swords with human faces were being carried as early as 1635. Not all of them display human faces as the primary decorative motif. Alternative hilt decoration comprises armed figures, coats of arms and extensive engraving, including both fanciful and geometric designs.

ABOVE A mid-17th century English backsword with a mortuary-type hilt. It was reputed to have been used by Oliver Cromwell during the siege of Drogheda in 1649.

The main features of the mortuary sword are a dish- or boat-shaped guard with a wide wrist guard and two branched knuckle bows screwed to the pommel. Shield-shaped langets (to guard the shaft) are found at the top of the blade forte and probably acted to keep the hilt solid into the blade. Blades were normally of backsword type and single or double-edged towards the end of the blade to enable a thrusting capability.

The mortuary sword, which fell out of use around 1670, was carried by both Royalist and Parliamentarian cavalry throughout the English Civil War. Oliver Cromwell was believed to have carried a mortuary sword during the Battle of Drogheda, in 1649, and an example attributed to him still exists in England.

BELOW Oliver Cromwell at the siege of Drogheda, 1649. Instead of starving the Royalist garrison into submission, Cromwell ordered an assault. This was eventually successful and led to a terrible massacre of both the military and civilians.

Brass "cat's-
head" pommel

BELOW A schiavona sword of a type carried by Slavonian soldiers who acted as guards to the Doge of Venice up until the late 18th century.

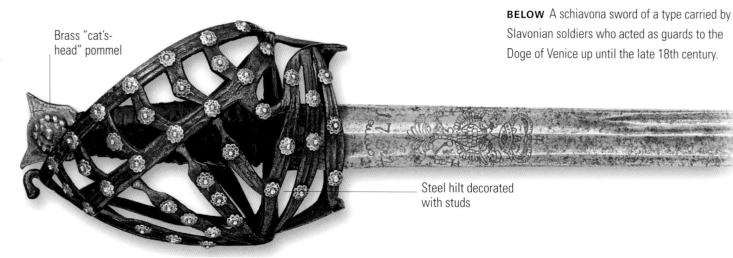

Steel hilt decorated
with studs

The schiavona

Slavonic mercenaries from eastern Europe, particularly the Balkan or Dalmatian region, carried distinctive broadswords and are thought to be the originators of the schiavona sword. These mercenaries were vicariously employed by both Spain and the Republic of Venice during the 16th and 17th centuries, but the schiavona is probably best known for its Venetian association. The Council of Ten, or Consiglio dei Dieci, under which the Doge (head of state) administered the Venetian state during the 1600s, hired many of these Dalmatian mercenaries to protect and promote Venetian interests. A large store of schiavona swords is still present in the Armoury of the Doge's Palace, in Venice. Most are stamped with the "CX" mark for the Consiglio dei Dieci.

The schiavona sword has a most distinctive hilt design. Hilt styles differ but they all exhibit the common feature of having a multi-leaf-shaped guard and "cat's-head", or katzenkopfknauf, pommel in either brass, bronze or

iron. Early examples are simpler in form with less complex basket hilts, whereas later schiavonas are usually of higher quality, with the hilt bars cast in one piece.

This particular sword proved popular with central and north European cavalry during the 17th and 18th centuries. Its long and wide blade was very effective as a slashing weapon, allowing the horseman both to cut and to thrust.

Hunting swords

The dedicated European hunting sword came into prominence during the mid-1600s. Its rise was attributed to the increasing use of firearms and the changing nature of the hunt. Now the hunting sword was used to dispatch wounded or exhausted game brought to bay by the hounds, rather than being the

BELOW The Council of Ten at the Doge's Palace, Venice, painted in the 18th century. The council hired mercenaries during the 17th and 18th centuries to fight for Spain and the Republic of Venice.

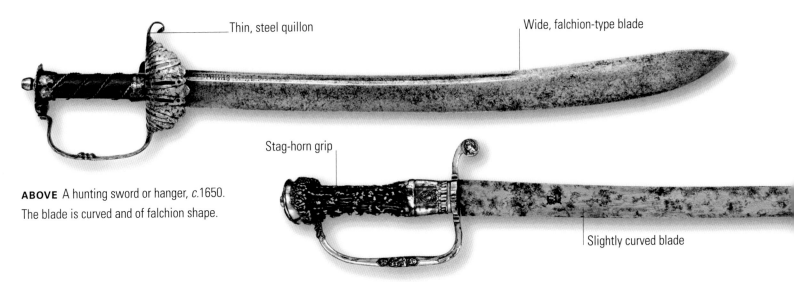

Thin, steel quillon

Wide, falchion-type blade

Stag-horn grip

ABOVE A hunting sword or hanger, c.1650. The blade is curved and of falchion shape.

Slightly curved blade

ABOVE The hilt of this hunting sword, 1650–75, is English, while the blade is German. The hilt is cast in hallmarked silver.

primary weapon of choice for the outright kill. Later, this sword would become more of an ornament than a functional weapon.

From around 1650, the most common form of hunting sword style was a short, lightweight hanger with a broad, single-edged, straight or sometimes slightly curved blade, typically no more than 64cm (25in) long. Some earlier blades had serrated back edges that could be used for sawing through bone.

Although hunting swords were used throughout western Europe, they were most popular in the German-speaking countries and France. Hunting swords were also referred to as hangers because they hung vertically from a sword belt, or baldric. German hunting swords are more commonly known as hirschfangers, which translates as "deer catchers".

Hunting sword hilts
Many different materials were incorporated into the construction of the hunting sword hilt, with a combination of two or three being quite common. Silver, brass, bronze, steel and later, silver was widely used. In England, silver was a popular metal for the manufacture of hunting sword hilts. The hilt would be cast in silver and then designs worked onto it, with prominent hallmarks stamped on the hilt, enabling identification of the maker and the place of manufacture.

Blade decoration
Although the hilts were furnished from many sources, the blade was normally obtained from Solingen, north-western Germany, which had a virtual monopoly on hunting sword blades from the 17th to the 19th century. Decoration of the blade usually took the form of an

etched or engraved design, including scenes of the hunt and related animal motifs. A gold wash or gilt finish would sometimes be applied over these designs. Towards the middle of the 18th century, both blue and gilt were commonly applied to the blades.

Sword scabbards and sword styles
The hunting sword scabbard was in itself a very skilled piece of work. Each scabbard was individually constructed and fitted to its own sword. Scabbards of the 17th century were normally made from thin, shaped pieces of wood, glued together to form a rigid base that would receive an external covering of parchment, calfskin or Morocco leather. Scabbard mounts included a metal locket at the upper end and a chape at the tip. A stud was also fixed to the locket that would be placed in the eye of a belt frog worn around the waist or over the shoulder.

Occasionally, a pocket was constructed in the locket mount, containing either a small knife or a fork. The handles on these tools were matched with the sword hilt and designed to complement the rest of the outfit to form a set, or trousse.

Through the 17th and into the first half of the 18th century, hunting swords became even more ornamental and were decorated in the Baroque style. Based on classical ideals, this was ebullient in spirit and characterized by rich decorative effects, including the use of prolific foliage, rounded contours and heavy symmetrical volutes. By the mid-18th century, the Rococo style had taken over and motifs based on shell and rock forms, foliage, flowers, "C" scrolls and tortuous curves were now in vogue.

Scottish Highlander swords

For centuries the Scottish Highlander fought with a distinctively Scottish range of weapons. Most notable were the broadsword, targe (small shield), dirk (dagger) and polearm. Over time the Highland broadsword eclipsed the others, both in its unique design and in the associated romance that has captured the imagination of many. It took many forms: from the massive two-handed claymore of the 16th century to the agile basket hilt, wielded at the Battle of Culloden in 1746.

Langet

Quatrefoils

ABOVE A claymore, *c.*1600. This large sword was the mainstay of the Highlander until the late 17th century.

16th- and 17th-century Highland swords

Before the introduction of a recognized basket hilt, the Scottish Highlander already carried at least three distinct sword types. The first comprised the claidheamh mor (claymore), which was a double-edged broadsword. Introduced during the 1500s, it was of hand-and-a-half length, with a long, broad blade of diamond section, with a cross guard angled towards the blade. The end of the cross guard was also decorated with brazed iron quatrefoils (four-leafed flower petals).

In the late 16th and early 17th centuries, Highlanders also carried the claidheamh da laimh, a two-handed sword. It was similar to contemporary German or Swiss two-handed (Zweihänder) swords used by Landsknechte, or mercenaries. The few surviving Scottish examples have Scottish hilts fitted with German blades. The hilt includes an oval shell guard and long, flattened, downswept quillons. The third sword type is referred to as the "lowland sword". It had a very long blade with a characteristic side ring to the hilt, globular pommel and quillons set at right angles to the blade, terminating in knobs. These great lowland swords were used for many years, and even as late as 1746, after the Battle of Culloden, many examples were subsequently found on the battlefield.

Origins of the Scottish basket hilt

The geographical origin of the distinctly "Scottish" basket-hilted sword was not actually Scotland. Swords with basket hilts are thought to have originated in Germany, Scandinavia and even England, where basket hilts of simple form were already known by the early 1500s. The development of an enclosed hilt was a natural consequence of the need for more protection to the hand at a time when the wearing of armour,

LEFT A Scottish Highlander with basket hilt and targe (shield) at the Battle of Culloden, 16 April 1746.

RIGHT **RIGHT** In this 17th-century oil painting of Mungo Murray (1668–1700), the fifth son of the Marquis of Athol, the subject is depicted as dressed for hunting in a costume of highland tartan. The sword he carries under his left arm is an early ribbon-hilted broadsword.

and particularly the metal gauntlet, had become less common. Why the sword became associated with Highland use is not clear, although it is known that numbers of Scottish mercenaries fought for the English in Ireland during the 16th century, and it is probable that basket-hilted swords were brought back to Scotland and their design copied by local sword makers. They were then known as "Irish" hilts by their English contemporaries.

The first true Scottish basket hilts

There are very few written or visual sources to enable us to determine exactly when the basket hilt began to be carried in the Highlands. The earliest known painting showing a Scottish clansman carrying this type of sword is recorded c.1690. The painting is of a Highland Chieftain by John Michael Wright (1617–94), and shows the subject carrying a broadsword with "beaknose" or ribbon hilt. This comprised a series of welded ribbon-like strips of metal drawn together to form a beak at the front of the basket. The "beaknose" hilt was a uniquely Highland style and differed from English basket hilts in that the pommel was of "coned form" as opposed to the English "apple" shape. Pommel shape is an important indicator of whether a basket hilt is either Scottish or English. A number of characteristic differences between the hilt styles of Scottish and English swords also began to emerge in the 1600s. English hilts tended to have thinner, more spaced, bars, whereas Scottish hilts adopted wider, rectangular plates to either side of the hilt, coupled with decorative heart-shaped piercing.

Highland feuds

The idea of Highland clansmen being compelled to fight each other to the death during a duel is not historically accurate. There were many feuds between rival clans and broadswords were normally employed to settle these quarrels. But they did not always result in the death of one opponent. It was enough for a swordsman to have drawn first blood. Rob Roy MacGregor (1671–1734), the famous Scottish patriot and folk hero, fought a duel with sword and targe just before his death. His opponent, Alasdair Steward of Invernahyle, won the duel with a cut to Rob Roy's arm.

Quillon

LEFT A basket-hilted broadsword, c.1860. This sword would have been carried by a sergeant (non-commisioned officer) of a Scottish Highland regiment.

Silk tassels

Heart-shaped piercings

Forward guard

Broad, double-edged blade

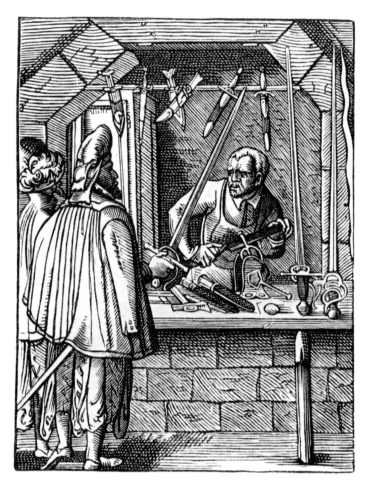

LEFT A European sword maker, *c.*1600. He is working on a sword hilt clamped within a vice. Around him are displayed daggers and rapiers.

prestigious title of King's Armourer in Scotland (1715), an honour carried on by his eldest son. This family of sword makers produced some very fine basket hilts, noted for their restrained elegance and fine detail.

The wide variety and breadth of quality that we see in Scottish basket hilts indicates that many were produced as part of a "cottage" industry. Most blades were actually imported from the continent, principally Germany and Italy, with the hilts then manufactured and decorated in Scotland. Small workshops in Glasgow, Stirling, Edinburgh and other Highland locations produced the swords with a workforce comprising little more than one or two people.

Post-Culloden and the banning of swords

After the failure of the Highland Scots to restore James Stuart (the Young Pretender) to the English throne at the Battle of Culloden in 1746, the Scottish Highlander lost his right to bear arms, and the carrying of swords was outlawed by the English Government. Most swords were not handed over to the English but hidden. The ban also had a devastating effect on Scottish sword makers, and the production of basket hilts went into steep decline. The subsequent raising of regiments for the newly established British Army in Scotland created a requirement for basic military broadswords. Ironically, most of these were actually

Scottish sword makers

We know of specific Highland makers only in instances where the maker has signed the hilt. Most Scottish-made basket hilts are unsigned, adding to the confusion of identification. Scottish sword makers are normally described as falling into two notable schools of basket-hilted sword making – that of either the "Stirling" or "Glasgow" schools. Edinburgh did manufacture basket hilts but not to the extent of Glasgow and Stirling. Swords of these schools are now acknowledged as representing the apogee of Scottish basket hilt sword making during the 18th century. The superb craftsmanship and detailing to the hilts identify them as being of truly historic form. Two sword-making families, the Simpsons and the Allans, predominated during this period.

During the first quarter of the 18th century, father and son hilt-makers (or "Hammermen") John Allan Sr and Walter Allan Jnr from Stirling produced hilts of rare artistry and freedom of style, many with intricately inlaid brass circles, wavy lines and cross hatching.

The Simpson family of Glasgow included a father and two sons, all confusingly named John. In 1683 the father was admitted as a Freeman of the Incorporation of Hammermen of Glasgow and was later conferred the

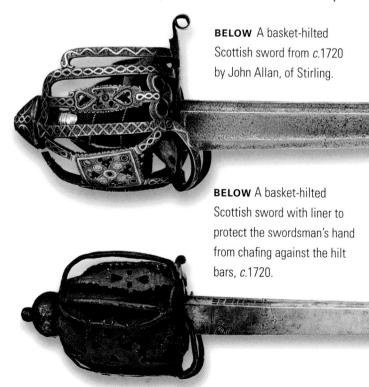

BELOW A basket-hilted Scottish sword from *c.*1720 by John Allan, of Stirling.

BELOW A basket-hilted Scottish sword with liner to protect the swordsman's hand from chafing against the hilt bars, *c.*1720.

The Highland charge

This account was written by Major General Hawley (c.1679–1759) before the Battle of Culloden and was meant to give the English soldiers a taste of what it would be like to face a mass charge of Highlanders.

They commonly form their Front rank of what they call their best men or True Highlanders, the number of which being always but few, when they form in Batallions they commonly form four deep...When these Battalions come within a large musket shott or three score yards this front rank gives their fire, and immediately throw down their firelocks and come down in a cluster with their swords and targets, making a noise and endeavouring to pierce the body or battalion before them – becoming 12 or 14 deep by the time they come up to the people they attack.

Records show that in most cases the enemy would have already fled the battlefield before the Highlanders reached them, but in the case of the Battle of Culloden the English forces had established complete military

ABOVE The Battle of Culloden, 16 April 1746. The army of Charles Edward Stuart (the Young Pretender) was swiftly crushed by William, Duke of Cumberland.

superiority, and could rely on the combined forces of the cavalry, infantry squares (armed with musket and fixed bayonet) and strategically placed artillery pieces.

No amount of heroic brute force could withstand this new form of military warfare. The Highlanders were unsurprisingly cut down in swathes.

produced in England. A basket-hilted sword for infantry privates in Highland regiments was issued c.1750–70. It was of relatively poor manufacture, with a thin sheet-metal guard and crude cut-outs in the junction plates. The grip was leather on wood. Blades were manufactured in London or Birmingham and marked with a royal "GR" crown, and the maker's name of either "Iefries" (Jeffries, London) or "Drury" (Birmingham). Most Scottish-made basket-hilted swords after 1746 are likely to have been made for officers in the newly formed Highland regiments.

In 1798, a regulation pattern of Highland Infantry Officer's basket-hilted broadsword was introduced. Its gilt brass basket hilt mirrored previous Highland designs. This pattern was replaced in 1828 by a basket hilt that is still worn by officers of Highland regiments in the British Army.

The Lochaber axe

First noted in the 1600s, the main polearm of the Highlander was the Lochaber axe. Its name derives from the Lochaber area of the Scottish Western Highlands. Agricultural in origin, it was similar to cropping tools such as the scythe. The pronounced

hook at the back of the axe could also have been used to pick up tied bundles. The axes ranged in height from 1.8–2m (5.9–6.5ft), including the haft.

This was a weapon carried extensively by Highland infantry and used primarily against massed cavalry. The axe hook allowed the Highlander to pull the cavalryman off his horse from where he could be swiftly dispatched with the thrusting, spiked end or axe blade.

ABOVE Re-enactors fighting with Lochaber axes and spears. The axes were heavy weapons, used by foot-soldiers for defence against cavalry and as a pike against infantry. The axe consisted of a wooden handle (haft) and a blade.

Napoleonic swords

Sword fighting during the Napoleonic Wars was primitive and brutish, typified by the thundering clash of opposing cavalry regiments and the hacking melee that followed. Unlike modern warfare, where military technology can quickly locate and kill at a distance, the Napoleonic swordsman was alongside his opponent and victim. Ironically, despite this battlefield butchery, the Napoleonic soldier lived in an age of Neo-classical and Romantic revival, in which elegant sword styles were matched by equally opulent uniforms.

British cavalry swords before 1796

Until the introduction of a universal sword for both light and heavy cavalry in 1788, the British Army had left the decision of which swords should be carried to individual colonels of regiments. Unsurprisingly, this led to a chaotic situation, with a plethora of sword types, many varying in both quality and effectiveness. Some unscrupulous colonels purchased cheap, substandard swords in the expectation of pocketing a profit from the deal and some regiments adopted swords that invariably broke on first contact with the enemy. This continual failing of blades during combat forced the authorities to establish a system of official government "proving", or testing, of blades. Eventually, a new series of officially approved cavalry sword patterns was introduced.

At this time, heavy cavalry regiments were issued a large iron or steel basket-hilted broadsword with a long, straight, broad-fullered blade. Military experience soon indicated that it was not a good design, with both officer and trooper versions badly balanced and cumbersome. The official system of blade inspection was still in its infancy and not all the blades were vigorously tested, so poor blade quality was still a major problem. The light cavalry version comprised a slightly curved blade and stirrup-shaped hilt. It was better received by troopers in the field as the curved blade proved effective at slashing on horseback.

The argument of whether a "cut" or "thrust" blade was most effective in battle would be continually debated within the British Army for the next 100 years, and many sword tests undertaken to establish the truth. This conundrum would not be properly resolved until 1908 when, with the introduction of the 1908 Pattern Cavalry Trooper's Sword, the British Army chose a thrusting rather than a cutting sword.

In 1796, two new sword designs were issued to officers and men. Blades were now subject to a more rigid official testing regime. A punched stamp with a crown and inspector's number was placed on the ricasso (the flat of the blade near the hilt) to indicate that a blade had been passed as suitable for use in combat.

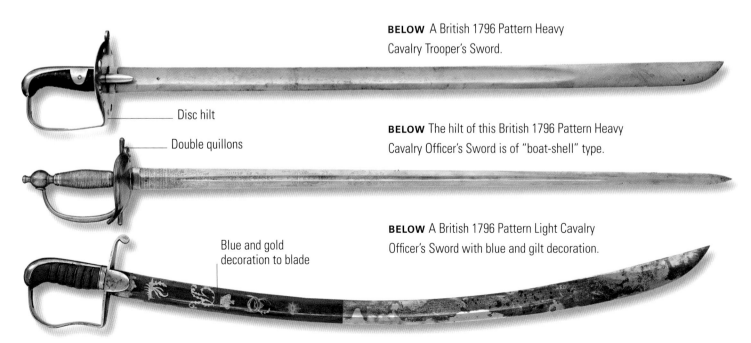

BELOW A British 1796 Pattern Heavy Cavalry Trooper's Sword.

Disc hilt

Double quillons

BELOW The hilt of this British 1796 Pattern Heavy Cavalry Officer's Sword is of "boat-shell" type.

BELOW A British 1796 Pattern Light Cavalry Officer's Sword with blue and gilt decoration.

Blue and gold decoration to blade

British cavalry swords after 1796

The 1796 Pattern Heavy Cavalry Trooper's Sword has found modern-day recognition as the sword favoured by Captain Richard Sharpe of the green-jacketed 95th Rifles Brigade, a colourful and dashing fictional character in the novels by Bernard Cornwell. The practical necessity for an infantry officer to carry such a long sword is a little far-fetched as the weapon

ABOVE The painting *Scotland for Ever*, by Lady Butler, shows the charge of the Royal Scots Greys at Waterloo in 1815. They are depicted carrying the 1796 Pattern Heavy Cavalry Trooper's Sword.

actually measured around 110cm (43.3in) from blade tip to top of the hilt, which would have made it quite a burden to drag around while on foot. The reality is that most rifle officers carried a stirrup-hilted and curved sabre of much smaller proportions.

One of the most famous real-life exponents of this pattern sword was Sergeant Charles Ewart of the 2nd Dragoons (Scots Greys), who captured the French Eagle at the Battle of Waterloo (1815). His later retelling of the act highlights the effectiveness of a large sabre when used in the right hands.

It was in the charge I took the eagle off the enemy; he and I had a hard contest for it; he made a thrust at my groin I parried it off and cut him down through the head. After this a lancer came at me; I threw the lance off my right side, and cut him through the chin upwards through the teeth. Next, a foot soldier fired at me, then charged me with his bayonet, which I also had the good luck to parry, and I cut him down through the head; thus ended the contest.

Sgt. Charles Ewart, 2nd Dragoons
(Scots Greys), Waterloo, 1815
from Edward Cotton, *A Voice from Waterloo* (1862)

The 1804 Birmingham sword trials

Driven by a heady mixture of technological pride and simple xenophobia, two Birmingham-based sword cutlers, James Woolley and Henry Osborn, were so certain of the superiority of their British-made sword blades that they agreed to a series of tests vying their blades against a number of imported German blades from Solingen that were currently being supplied to the British Army. On 7 November 1804, the tests were conducted under the supervision of a Major Cunningham. Predictably (and no doubt foreknown by Woolley and Osborn), the Solingen blades failed in droves, with many of them snapping immediately upon being struck against iron plates or when bent with any force. Both Woolley and Osborn went on to become major suppliers of military swords to the British Army throughout the Napoleonic Wars.

French cavalry swords

The rise of Napoleon Bonaparte coincided with a great revival and interest in the ancient classical world, particularly its architecture and decoration. This creative mood was not lost on French sword makers and Napoleon, who also understood the morale-boosting effect of appearance in his army. This resulted in many new cavalry sword designs being introduced during this period. One of the most influential designs was the AN XIII Heavy Cuirassier Trooper's Sword. It was a very heavy sword, with a four-bar brass hilt and a long, straight, single-edged blade measuring around 95cm (37.4in). It was a fearsome sword when used as a thrusting weapon (almost like a small spear) causing more fatal injuries than the hatchet-bladed and slashing swords of the British cavalry regiments. A French eyewitness recounts the effectiveness of these spear pointed blades but also acknowledges that when a British blade found its mark it could be equally devastating:

We always thrust with the point of our sabres, whereas they always cut with their blade which was three inches wide. Consequently, out of every twenty blows aimed by them, nineteen missed. If, however, the edge of the blade found its mark only once, it was a terrible blow, and it was not unusual to see an arm cut clean from the body.

Captain Charles Parquin, "*Chasseurs à Cheval of the Imperial Guard*"
from Charles Parquin, *Military Memoirs*, ed. (1969)

The French light cavalry trooper carried an elegant three-bar, brass-hilted sword with slightly curved blade, with hussar regiments favouring a stirrup-hilted sword. Elite regiments such as the Imperial Guard Dragoons carried a fine broadsword with brass basket hilt, cap pommel and a hilt with an inset oval plate and a silver or brass flaming grenade badge. The Mousquetaires de la Garde du Roi, who served as the mounted bodyguard to Louis XVIII

(*r.*1814–24) after Napoleon abdicated his throne in 1814, used an equally elegant sword. It was similar to the Imperial Guard Dragoon's sword, but with a cross, fleur-de-lys and sun ray inset within the hilt.

The manufacture of French swords

Swords issued by the government to French cavalry troopers were normally marked on the spine of the blade with the year, month and place of manufacture. From the 1700s, the town of Klingenthal, in Alsace, eastern France, became the official government location for the manufacture of French military

ABOVE In this illustration, *c.*1790, entitled *Officier de Cuirassiers de la Garde Royale*, you can see the sword knot hanging from the sword hilt. It prevented the sword from slipping out of the hand.

Four-bar hilt

ABOVE French Heavy Cuirassier Trooper's Sword, *c.*1810. It was used primarily as a thrusting weapon.

Flattened diamond section
with narrow fuller

ABOVE Small officer's sword, dated 1780, presented to Napoleon by a friend and comrade who attended military school with him.

swords. It produced an enormous quantity of swords, both before and after the French Revolution. Blades produced during the period of Louis XVIII's monarchy are marked to the spine with a designation of "Rle" (Royal). Those manufactured during the reign of Napoleon are marked with the designation "Imple" (Imperial). After the Napoleonic Wars (1799–1815), French sword hilts and blades were constantly re-used and many Napoleonic era blades were fitted on new hilts well into the 19th century.

Clam or fan-shaped
hilt guard

ABOVE Note the fan-shaped hilt guard on this French Napoleonic Heavy Cavalry Officer's Sword from *c.*1800.

The mameluke sword

During the Egyptian campaigns of 1798–1801, the French army was greatly influenced by its military contact with the opposing Mamluk slave troops of the Ottoman (Turkish) Empire. Dressed in colourful robes and armed with pistol, daggers and distinctively curved scimitars, the Mamluks soon caught the attention of many French officers, who quickly adopted their scimitars, now renamed mamelukes, as part of their military uniform.

Evidence of the vogue for mameluke swords amongst French officers is found in the famous painting of *The Battle of the Pyramids* (1810) by Antoine-Jean Gros (1771–1835), in which he depicts *all* of the French officers carrying mameluke swords. Napoleon was so impressed with the fighting spirit of the Mamluks that he went on to purchase 2,000 troops from Syrian merchants, raising a regiment of "Mamelukes", who eventually served in his Imperial Guard. Napoleon also chose a Mamluk (Roustam Raza) to be his personal bodyguard. The mameluke sword was also adopted by British officers, and its influence even spread to the burgeoning United States, where

Marine Lieutenant Francis O'Bannion was presented with a scimitar for his capture of Derne (modern-day Tripoli) in 1804, the first recorded land battle of the US Army on foreign soil.

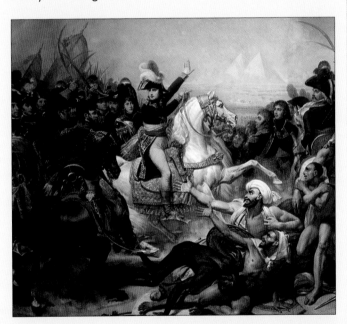

ABOVE The victorious French officers at the battle of the Pyramids, 21 July 1798, are all carrying mameluke swords.

RIGHT The mameluke sword presented to Marine Lieutenant Francis O'Bannion, in recognition of his leadership and success during the capture of Tripoli, 1804.

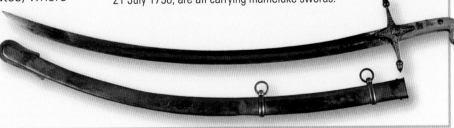

British infantry swords

Officers did not carry an officially approved regulation sword until 1786. Before this, an officer chose his own sword and most opted for variations of the popular narrow-bladed smallsword. Some also opted for short hangers with flat-backed blades.

1786 Pattern Infantry Officer's Sword

Following an Order issued by George III (1738–1820), the 1786 Pattern Infantry Officer's Sword was introduced. The Order stipulated that this new sword pattern must be:

...strong cut and thrust weapon with blade 32in long and 1in wide at the shoulder, the hilt to be steel, gilt or silver according to the buttons of the uniform.

Grips were composed of either ribbed ivory, ebony or dark horn, with some swords having a metal "cigar band" placed around the centre of the grip. This normally bore an engraved royal crown, the "GR" cypher of George III, or even a regimental badge. Hilts had a cushion-shaped pommel and forward knuckle bow with five decorative balls, or "beads". These beads are sometimes found on the side guard.

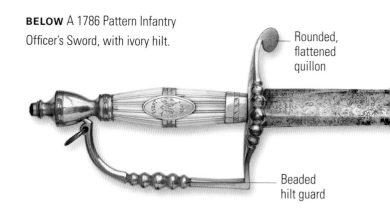

BELOW A 1786 Pattern Infantry Officer's Sword, with ivory hilt.

Rounded, flattened quillon

Beaded hilt guard

Later versions featured a fixed double-shell guard and "Adam style" urn pommel (from the Neo-classical architect Robert Adam, 1728–1792). Both pommel and quillon were decorated with acanthus leaves.

1796 Pattern Infantry Officer's Sword

The disparate hilt variations were finally standardized in the 1796 Pattern Infantry Officer's Sword, a weapon that epitomized the British Napoleonic Infantry Officer's sword. The original inspiration for the design came from Prussian military smallswords of the 1750s. Upon close inspection, it is clear that this rather flimsy bladed sword would not have stood up to a charging horseman's broadsword or sabre, but these were times

Sword wounds

Ironically, a clean sword cut received during battle probably gave you more chance of survival than a wound caused by a musket ball or artillery. This is because the steel blade was less likely to contain deadly infected matter that could be driven into the body by the discharge of a firearm. Surgeons also found sword wounds easier to treat through cauterization, and consequently patients were less likely to suffer the effects of gangrene and post-operative infection. Although a cut from a sword could undoubtedly inflict dreadful wounds, there are many tales of soldiers receiving multiple sword wounds and still surviving. At the Battle of Waterloo (1815), the French divisional commander, General Pierre-François Durette, of the Fourth Corps, lost his hand to a sword cut and also received life-threatening cuts to the face and head, leading to blindness in one eye. Remarkably, he survived these awful injuries and lived on until 1862.

LEFT The Battle of Waterloo, 18 June 1815. Napoleon is depicted with sword aloft rallying his men, including the Imperial Guard (on the right of the image).

The hussars of eastern Europe

A common image in both British and French art of this period, and also found engraved on many sword blades, is the sight of a dashing hussar, sword held aloft. The word *hussar* is Hungarian in origin and loosely

translated means "highwayman" or "brigand", but was later used to describe a lightly armed horseman. Hungarian and Polish-Lithuanian hussars of the 17th and 18th centuries were utilized as shock troops during constant wars with the Ottoman Empire in eastern Europe and the Balkans. They carried both curved and straight-bladed swords. Importantly, Polish hussars also retained the lance and were largely responsible for its re-introduction during the Napoleonic Wars. Napoleon formed his own Imperial Guard regiment of lancers in 1810, known as the Red Lancers. They fought with distinction in the Russian campaign of 1812 and the Battle of Waterloo in 1815. Their lances were around 2.74m (9ft) long with a fluted steel point, mounted on a wooden shaft.

LEFT The swords carried by hussars inspired the curved sabres adopted by British light cavalry regiments of the early 19th century.

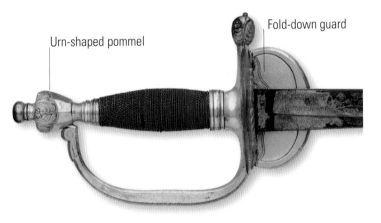

Urn-shaped pommel

Fold-down guard

LEFT A 1796 Pattern Infantry Officer's Sword, with folding shell guard.

1803 Pattern Infantry Officer's Sword

The colourful image of the gallant and dashing light cavalryman or hussar had created a strong impetus within British light cavalry regiments to carry a curved or "hussar" sabre that reflected this new *esprit de corps*. Not to be outdone, the infantry regiments introduced a new pattern of sword based on contemporary light cavalry swords.

when elegant appearance sometimes took precedence over practicality. Protection for the hand was minimal, with just a single knuckle guard and double shell guard. One of the shell guards was hinged in order that it could be folded and so prevent chafing by the uniform. The grip was bound in either silver wire or applied sheet silver. Blades were lavishly decorated with blue-and-gilt highlighted engraving.

The 1803 Pattern Infantry Officer's Sword had a single-edged, curved blade with a lion's-head pommel and a gilt brass knuckle bow. A "GR" royal cypher and crown were affixed within the knuckle bow, and above that was a representation of either a strung bugle, denoting use by a rifle company officer, or a flaming grenade, symbolizing a grenadier company officer. The blade was usually decorated in blue and gilt.

Lion's-head pommel

Openwork guard

Flat-backed blade

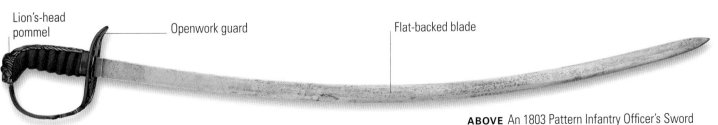

ABOVE An 1803 Pattern Infantry Officer's Sword with a lion's-head pommel.

ABOVE Napoleon bids farewell to the Imperial Guard at Fontainebleau in April 1814, after his first abdication and prior to his exile in Elba. The following year he was to lose the Battle of Waterloo.

French infantry swords

Napoleon Bonaparte's armies displayed a far greater range of infantry swords than most of their European counterparts. The perceived importance of rank and regiment was highly regarded within the French Army and we find that an infantry private, sergeant, captain and general officer all carried their own specific model of sword. The early years after the French Revolution (1789–99) saw the development of many distinctive infantry swords, including those carried by prestigious regiments such as the Garde Nationale and Garde Nationale Chasseur. These unique swords featured Neo-classical helmet pommels and half-basket brass guards with republican emblems (such as the Phrygian cap) placed within the hilt cartouche.

A common type of sword carried by French infantry privates during the Napoleonic Wars was the sabre briquet, which was a short, brass-hilted hanger. It comprised a slightly curved, single-edged, flat-backed blade with brass and leather mounted scabbard. This sword was widely copied throughout Europe and adopted by many countries during the early to mid-1800s. Napoleon also understood the importance of rewarding his favoured regiments with honours or special uniform and equipment privileges. This beneficence also applied to swords. An example of this is the distinctive sword of the Imperial Sappers (Pioneers) of the Old Guard. They were awarded a newly designed uniform including bearskin, felling axe, apron and, more importantly, a striking, cockerel-hilted sword. They were also granted the unique right to grow a beard.

French infantry smallswords and curved sabres

Throughout the 18th century, French infantry officers had always carried a straight-bladed sword. It usually took the form of a traditional smallsword, with pommel styles ranging from plain ovoid to Neo-classical helmet. Shell guards were also classically inspired, with some featuring extensive embossed decoration including victory wreaths, stands of trophies and figures in classical poses.

This style continued throughout the Napoleonic Wars and blades were also frequently finished in blue and gilt. The vogue for Neo-classical hilts and corresponding decoration to the blade influenced the design of other infantry swords, including a wide range of curved infantry sabres, similar to their light cavalry counterparts but with shorter and lighter blades. There was little official pressure formally to regulate these swords and French officers were allowed a great deal of freedom to choose whatever style of sword they wished to carry.

Blue and gilt decoration

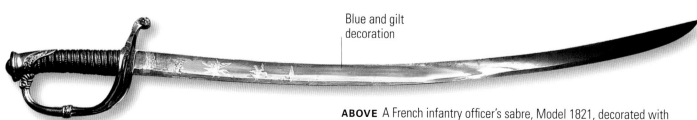

ABOVE A French infantry officer's sabre, Model 1821, decorated with blue and gilt. This form of decoration was beginning to lose favour and later examples have plain blades.

Russian infantry swords

From the mid-1700s, Russia embarked on a sustained period of contact and rapprochement with the West. These new influences hastened changes in civil administration, architectural styles, dress and, most importantly, military organization. The czars had looked with envy at the disciplined troops of Frederick the Great of Prussia (1712–1786) and wanted the same attitude to be instilled within their own ranks. To do this the czars needed to change the whole appearance of the Russian army which, it was hoped, would then improve the military effectiveness of both the officers and rank and file. One of the methods of achieving this goal was to adopt Western military dress and weapons.

By 1800, the Russian infantry officer was carrying a smallsword of European style. The Model 1786 Infantry Officer's Sword had a slightly curved, double-edged blade with a brass, heart-shaped guard and ovoid pommel. It was contained within a leather and brass mounted scabbard. Subsequent patterns (Model 1796 and Model 1798) had straight, single-edged blades with typical Napoleonic double shell guards and pronounced upward quillons.

Lower ranks in the infantry carried simple brass-hilted short swords with shell guards. As the century progressed, the Russian infantry adopted the same style of brass-hilted hanger as that carried by Prussian and English troops.

German infantry swords

The German states of the 18th and 19th centuries normally followed the sword patterns and styles prevalent throughout Europe. In keeping with French and English infantry privates of the mid- to late-1700s, a short, brass-hilted infantry hanger was carried throughout the Napoleonic Wars, particularly by Prussian infantrymen.

By 1800, German officers were already wearing a sword similar in design to the British 1796 Pattern Infantry Officer's Sword (the British had actually copied the pattern from a Prussian design of the 1750s). Hilt design was also heavily influenced by French infantry swords of the period. Sword blades featured engraved decoration, including the coats of arms and royal cyphers of individual states. Blue and gilt were also used extensively. There was no real attempt at uniformity of pattern, and different German states adopted and jealously guarded their own styles of infantry sword.

Austro-Hungarian infantry swords

The Austro-Hungarian infantry officer of the 1800s followed the same path as his British and German counterparts in favouring a smallsword. It included a gilt brass hilt with double boat shell guard and rounded pommel. The blade was straight and double-edged. Blades were normally engraved with the royal cypher and double-headed eagle of the Habsburg monarchy. Austrian infantry officers also carried a wide range of unofficial swords, including wide-bladed and curved "hussar"-type sabres. This type of sword was popular with infantry regiments throughout Europe during the 19th century.

Wide, hatchet-point blade

ABOVE An Austrian hussar's sword. The blade is unusually wide, and single-edged with a hatchet point.

Boat-shaped hilt

Double-edged blade

ABOVE An Austro-Hungarian infantry officer's sword from c.1800. It has a double-edged blade with a double boat shell guard and rounded pommel.

The American sword

At the start of the American War of Independence (1775–83) the opposing armies carried a very similar range of weapons. This was inevitable because the Continental Army of General George Washington (1732–99) included many former British-trained local militias, armed with both British government and their own privately purchased weapons. As the war progressed and the British blockade of ports such as Boston (1775) began to bite, American forces had difficulty sourcing weapons from overseas. This forced them to rely on simple, locally manufactured swords, leading to the adoption of a distinctly "American" sword style.

Colonists' swords in the 16th and 17th centuries

The early settlers of the 16th and 17th centuries, living in newly established colonies such as Virginia and New England, were predominantly of British stock and brought with them significant quantities of edged weapons, particularly swords. Contemporary records of the period and subsequently excavated examples indicate that rapiers, short hangers and long-bladed horsemen's sabres were the most common sword types of this period. Apart from swords brought

directly from England or purchased from passing trading ships, a number of simple, locally forged swords were also manufactured in the colonies.

The American colonies were a crucial part of the expanding empires of both Great Britain and France, so a regular military presence was required to maintain order and promote national interests. During the early 18th century, soldiers from these nations carried the same swords in the colonies as they would have done in their home countries, including short, brass-hilted hangers for infantry troops and short hangers or smallswords for the officers.

The American War of Independence

During the early years of the American War of Independence the colonists fighting against the British and her allies would have carried virtually identical swords to their enemies. Later in the war, when replacements became more difficult to source from overseas, the colonists turned towards domestically manufactured weapons to fill the shortfall. Local American blacksmiths forged simple military blades that were attached to improvised hilts.

Although these blades were never produced to impress (tending to be flat, unfullered and undecorated), they proved quite effective on the battlefield. In the absence of any official style or designated sword patterns for the new Continental Army, American sword makers merely copied or interpreted the British or French patterns available at that time. The main priority of the Continental Army was to produce swords and edged weapons as quickly as possible.

LEFT The surrender of the British General Cornwallis, Yorktown, 1781. It was a tradition that the defeated commanding officer handed over his sword to the victor.

Cavalry swords in the 18th century

American cavalry troops of the 1770s carried an assortment of swords, including long, straight-bladed, basket-hilted broadswords and light cavalry sabres. Many would have been captured from the British. Their armoury also included home-made "D-guard", slotted-hilt, and flat-bladed backswords with simple, turned wooden grips. Typical pommel shapes such as ball, urn, cap, ovoid, high domed, flat or lion's head were also used. Scabbards were manufactured in leather and wood, with crude iron mounts.

Infantry swords in the 18th century

The ordinary American infantry soldier and officer of the 1770s had an extensive range of weapons, many of them captured from the British and some home-produced. The short hanger or hunting sword was favoured by the infantry officer, especially when fighting in the dense forests of North America, where a long-bladed sword was sometimes impractical. Smallswords were also carried by American officers but it is unlikely they would have been the first weapon of choice for combat.

Sword types after the War of Independence

During the War of Independence, the Eagle Pommel Sword became one of the defining "American" sword types of this period. It remained popular after the war.

In the 1800s, many of these swords were supplied to American officers by British-based sword makers, most notably William Ketland and Henry Osborn of Birmingham. In America, Frederick W. Widmann, a German-born sword maker, made distinctive and high-quality Eagle Pommel Swords in Philadelphia during the 1830s and 1840s. Indian-head and Neo-classical helmet pommels were also very popular during this period. Blade decoration began to incorporate specifically nationalistic American themes.

The new cavalry sword of 1798

After independence, the new American government began to form its fledgling army into established regiments, and with this reorganization there was the requirement to arm troops with new swords. The American Congress did not want to rely solely on overseas countries for their swords and so a domestic manufacturer was actively sought for a new model of cavalry sword. Nathan Starr, of Middleton, Connecticut, initially produced 2,000 Model 1798 Cavalry Trooper's Swords.

The sword had a simple stirrup guard with a leather and wood-covered grip, and a single-edged, slightly curved blade. The blade was marked "N Starr & Co." on one side and "US – 1799" on the other. Starr produced updated versions of this sword between 1814 and 1818.

The "Eagle Pommel Sword"

A common weapon of the post-Revolutionary War period was the American "Eagle Pommel Sword". During the war, other animal forms were also used for the pommel, including horses', dogs' and lions' heads. The variety of hilt and pommel types produced by American sword makers is numerous, and they were manufactured in silver, brass and iron, with grips of ivory, horn, wood and leather. They also differed widely in terms of quality and construction, reflecting the challenging conditions and the scarcity of basic materials. The sword makers were usually imitating British and continental sword styles of the period, but the relative naivety of design and crude construction of some types can be differentiated as typically "American". Conversely, there were also many American-made swords of this period that exhibited excellent workmanship.

ABOVE The American Eagle Pommel Sword was used by American officers. Early swords were normally produced in England.

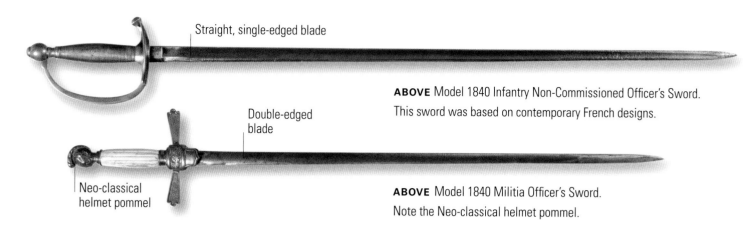

Straight, single-edged blade

Double-edged blade

Neo-classical helmet pommel

ABOVE Model 1840 Infantry Non-Commissioned Officer's Sword. This sword was based on contemporary French designs.

ABOVE Model 1840 Militia Officer's Sword. Note the Neo-classical helmet pommel.

By 1833, the N.P. Ames Sword Company of Springfield, Massachusetts, was manufacturing a robust brass, three-bar hilted cavalry sword with slightly curved blade. It was not well received by soldiers and, in 1840, the company introduced a cavalry trooper's sword of French style. This had a heavy, three-bar, brass hilt and a slightly curved blade with steel scabbard. It was grudgingly known by its users as the "wristbreaker".

This sword was replaced again in 1860 by a much lighter version, which became the standard issue cavalry trooper's sword for Union troops throughout the American Civil War (1861–65). The sword was updated in 1872 and 1906. Officers carried more elaborate versions with etched blades and embossed and gilt-covered hilts.

Infantry swords after 1830

Regulation infantry swords for the US Army began to appear from the 1830s. In 1832, a rather impractical smallsword of English style, with a gilt-brass boat-shell hilt, ovoid pommel and straight blade was introduced for officers of the Infantry, Artillery and Ordnance. There followed a number of other regulation infantry swords including the Model 1840 Foot Officer's Sword, similar to the Non-Commissioned Officer's version. The blade was straight, single-edged, with a double fuller. Decoration included drums, cannons, floral sprays, "US", eagles and crossed military pikes.

During the 1840s, states raised their own militias, and officers were required to provide their own uniform and sword. This gave them the opportunity to choose from a wide variety of swords from private manufacturers. Differences of design normally centred on the pommel type and blade decoration. Some have Neo-classical helmet pommels in the style of contemporary French infantry swords, and other examples feature diverse interpretations of the American eagle-head pommel.

Militia regiments were also keen to present swords to fellow officers, and some presentation-grade swords are truly spectacular, with grips of engraved brass, silver or even gold, with heavy embossed decoration to the hilt and scabbard mounts. A number of swords were decorated over the entire length of the blade. The regular US Army also carried sword patterns specific to individual departments or branches of service. These included the Model 1834 Revenue Cutter Service Sword; the Model 1840 Engineer's Sword; the Model 1840 Commissary Officer's Sword; and the Model 1832 and Model 1840 Medical Staff Officer's Sword.

Infantry swords after 1850

In the mid-19th century and in keeping with the vogue for French-inspired designs, the US Army introduced a completely new sword for infantry officers. The Model 1850 Foot Officer's Sword is an almost exact copy of the French Model 1845 Infantry Officer's Sword. The blade is slightly curved and single edged, with double fullers. Decoration took the form of an outstretched American Eagle, floral and military motifs, "US" and the US government motto

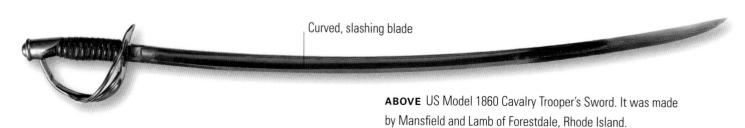

Curved, slashing blade

ABOVE US Model 1860 Cavalry Trooper's Sword. It was made by Mansfield and Lamb of Forestdale, Rhode Island.

Confederate swords in the American Civil War (1861–65)

Prior to the American Civil War, the US Army was composed of officers and men from both the Southern and Northern states. In general, they carried the same sword models and this continued until war between the Union and Confederacy was declared on 12 April 1861.

During the early days of the war, many Confederate officers still carried their original Union swords but, as the war dragged on and the Union undertook a successful blockade of southern ports, overseas sword imports to the South began to dry up. Some imports still got through and Confederate agents were constantly busy in Europe, sourcing swords from both Britain and Germany, but this was still not enough to furnish a growing Confederate army and to replace the loss of existing swords due to combat. Confederate officers also wanted to differentiate themselves from the enemy and carry swords that reflected their national aspirations. This meant that the Confederate government was forced to turn to local manufacturers to make up the shortfall.

Southern sword makers usually copied the Union sword patterns, but there were subtle changes. These included the replacement of the standard "US" lettering on sword hilts with a "CS" or "CSA", representing the Confederate States or Confederate

BELOW Confederate Cavalry Officer's Sword, *c.*1864. Standards of manufacture in the north were invariably superior.

ABOVE William Tecumseh Sherman (1820–91) left, Union general, meeting General Joseph E. Johnston (Confederate) to discuss terms of surrender of Confederate forces in North Carolina, 24 April 1865.

States of America. Blade etching also included specifically Southern motifs, including the five-pointed star of the Confederacy or a circle of 11 stars, which represented the 11 Confederate states.

However, most Southern sword makers, working with basic machinery and lacking essential raw materials, were forced to produce rather crudely manufactured swords. The quality deteriorated even further as a number of established Southern sword-making factories were overrun by Union forces towards the end of the war.

Crudely cast hilt

E Pluribus Unum (Out of Many, One). A large number of these swords were imported from Europe at the beginning of the American Civil War to make up for a shortfall in home production.

The Model 1850 Staff and Field Officer's Sword is similar to the Model 1850 Foot Officer except that it has an additional branch to the hilt, with a "US" set between the hilt bars. This was one of the most popular officer's swords carried by line officers and staff officers between 1850 and 1872.

Cavalry swords in the 20th century
The Model 1913 "Patton" hilt Cavalry Trooper's Sword was based on a design presented by the young Lieutenant George S. Patton (1885–1945) of the US Army, later to become a famous American general during World War II. This sword owes more than a passing nod to the popular British 1908 Pattern Cavalry Trooper's Sword but it differs in having a dove-head pommel, slightly lower basket guard and a wider, double-fullered blade.

Post-Napoleonic swords

The massed cavalry charges of the Napoleonic Wars had been a vital shock tactic, however, as the 19th century progressed, their effectiveness began to be questioned, especially in light of the huge advances being made in military technology. The contest between bullet and blade had now become one-sided. In the American Civil War, only 2 per cent of wounds received were from edged weapons. Nonetheless, the sword was still regarded as an essential combat weapon, and efforts were redoubled to design the perfect sword.

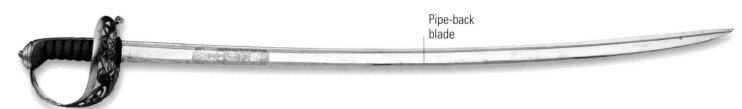

Pipe-back blade

ABOVE British 1821 Pattern Heavy Cavalry Officer's Sword with pipe-back (tubular) blade.

British light and heavy cavalry swords

Following the Napoleonic Wars, the British Army introduced a series of cavalry swords with both cut and thrust capabilities. These included the 1821 Pattern Light and Heavy Cavalry Trooper and Officer's swords. The light cavalry version comprised a steel, three-bar hilt and slightly curved, spear-point blade. Heavy cavalry officers also carried a spear-point blade, etched for most of its length, with a pierced bowl guard of acanthus-leafed decoration. Heavy cavalry troopers had a plain, solid bowl guard. The initial reception of these swords by troops in the field was poor, with frequent complaints that blades were too thin and liable to snap in combat. Soldiers also encountered difficulties when attempting to pierce enemy uniforms with their sword points, especially during the Crimean War (1853–56), when the Russian infantryman's thick greatcoat, combined with a rolled blanket worn on his back, made penetration by the blade extremely difficult.

The British universal pattern of 1853

In 1853, the next major change in British sword design occurred, when the differentiation between heavy and light cavalry troopers' swords was finally dropped in favour of a universal pattern. This was the 1853 Pattern Cavalry Trooper's Sword. It had the same three-bar hilt and blade as the previous 1821 pattern but employed a new "patent" grip, designed by the sword maker Charles Reeves, in partnership with fellow sword maker Henry Wilkinson. It was a revolutionary hilt design as it enabled the full width of the tang to be driven the length of the grip, rather than the previously tapered and potentially weaker tangs. Chequered leather grips were then riveted through this full-length tang, adding more strength and durability.

Thrusting versus cutting swords

From the mid-19th century, British cavalry swords went through a further series of changes. The historic argument concerning the use of either a thrusting or a cutting sword continued, with many official army committees established to consider the question. The eventual result of this "decision by committee" process was a predictably unsuitable compromise, with blades being neither fully straight to enable proper thrusting

Riveted grip

Spear-point blade

ABOVE British 1899 Pattern Cavalry Trooper's Sword with a slightly curved, spear-point blade.

The charge of the 21st Lancers, Battle of Omdurman, 1898

During the Second Sudan War, the Battle of Omdurman in 1898 was one of the last occasions when massed British cavalry carrying lances charged in force at the enemy. The future British prime minister, Winston Churchill, was present at the battle as a young cavalry officer attached to the 21st Lancers and he later graphically described his first-hand experiences on 2 September 1898. The sight of the 21st Lancers just before the famous charge was caught by Churchill in typically realistic terms:

…a great square block of ungainly figures and little horses, hung all over with water-bottles, saddle bags, picketing gear, tins of bully beef, all jolting and jangling together; the polish of peace gone; soldiers without glitter; horsemen without grace; but still a regiment of light cavalry in active service against the enemy…

from Winston Spencer Churchill, *The River War: An Historical Account of the Reconquest of the Soudan*, 2 Vols., ed. Col. F. Rhodes (Longmans, Green, London, 1899).

RIGHT Charge of the 21st Lancers at Omdurman, 2 September 1898. The battle was seen as Britain's revenge for the death of General Gordon at Khartoum, 1885. The charge of the 21st Lancers was regarded as the last full cavalry charge of a British regiment equipped with lances.

Colonel R.M. Martin, commanding officer of the 21st Lancers, initially engaged his 300 lancers with what appeared to be a few hundred Dervishes from the army of Abdullah al-Taashi (successor to the so-called "Mad Mahdi" Muhammad Ahmed, responsible for the death of General Gordon at Khartoum in 1885). But within seconds, over 2,000 spearmen and swordsmen crouching in a nearby shallow depression had risen to meet the advancing lancers. Having committed the regiment to the charge and too close to wheel around, Martin and his lancers crashed into the waiting Dervishes. Later accounts highlight the sheer brutality and bloodshed experienced during these colonial encounters. For their gallant action against impossible odds and driving back the Dervishes, three Victoria Crosses (the highest award for gallantry in the British Army) were subsequently awarded to members of the 21st Lancers. Their losses were five officers, 65 men, and 120 horses.

nor sufficiently curved for effective cutting. The patterns of 1864, 1882, 1885, 1890 and 1899 highlight the constant changes made to cavalry swords during this period in order to achieve this requirement.

British infantry swords

The Napoleonic 1796 and 1803 Pattern Infantry Officers' swords had a relatively long service life, and it was not until 1822 that a new pattern replaced them. This was very different in design to its predecessors and featured a "pipe-back" blade with a tubular sectioned back, or spine, to provide extra strength, combined with a "Gothic" gilt brass, half-basket hilt. The term "Gothic" refers to the similarity of the hilt profile to medieval Gothic church windows, the design of which heavily influenced the Gothic Revival in Britain during the first half of the 19th century. Within the hilt there was placed a "cartouche", or inset panel, featuring a cut-out royal cypher of the reigning monarch: for example, "VR" for "Victoria Regina".

British infantry swords in the late 19th century

The blue and gilt blade decoration favoured by a previous generation of British infantry officers had now become unfashionable, and blades were acid etched (rather than engraved) on a plain background.

Scabbards were leather and gilt brass mounted (for dress), brass or plain steel. The updated 1845 Pattern removed the folding guard, and the original pipe-back blade was replaced in the 1850s by a single-fullered "Wilkinson", spear-point blade that proved less prone to breaking.

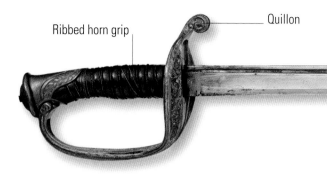

Ribbed horn grip — Quillon

ABOVE French Model 1845 Pattern Infantry Officer's Sword. This pattern would have been carried during the Crimean War (1853–56).

In 1892, the blade changed to a "dumb-bell" profile and became a purely thrusting weapon. There was also a complete redesign of the hilt which now took the form of a solid sheet steel, half-basket guard impressed or pierced with the Victorian royal crown and cypher. In 1895 and 1897, there were minor modifications to the hilt, including the addition of a turned-down inner edge to avoid fraying the officer's uniform.

The Rifle and Foot Guards regiments carried a steel half-basket-hilted sword (1827 Pattern and 1854 Pattern) of similar design to the 1822 Pattern "Gothic" hilt but with the addition of their regimental badges within the

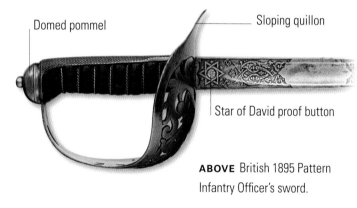

Domed pommel — Sloping quillon

Star of David proof button

ABOVE British 1895 Pattern Infantry Officer's sword.

ABOVE French Model 1845 Pattern Infantry Officer's Sword. This pattern would have been carried during the Crimean War (1853–56).

hilt. In 1857, the Royal Engineers were designated a pierced gilt-brass, half-basket-hilted sword which they carried until 1892, when they reverted to the standard 1897 Pattern Sword for all infantry officers.

French infantry swords

The French Model 1821 and 1845 Infantry Officer's Sword was a radical departure from previous infantry swords, and its elegant design inspired many other countries, particularly the United States. It comprised a decorated brass, half-basket hilt with a single knuckle bow guard and a slightly curved, single-edged, quill point blade. Grips were of ribbed horn and brass twistwire. The later Model 1845 continued the knuckle bow into a pierced shell guard with floral decoration. The blade was also a little straighter and produced in both pipe-back and quill-pointed form. Scabbards were leather and gilt-brass mounted. In 1855, the blade was changed to a single-fullered, spear-point type. This sword was carried until 1882, when the French Army introduced a nickel-plated steel, four-bar hilted sword with a much narrower, straight blade.

French sword design

In 1822, a new light cavalry sword was issued to French cavalry troopers. It comprised a three-bar brass hilt, slightly curved blade, and heavy steel scabbard. It would be adopted by many other countries during the 19th century. This was also true of the French Model 1829 Mounted Artillery Sword that featured a single "D-guard", brass knuckle bow and unusual, slightly domed pommel. This style of sword was copied by the United States (Model

1840 Artillery Officer's Sword) and carried throughout the American Civil War by Union forces. Other European nations such as Spain, Germany, Belgium and even Russia were all heavily influenced by French three or four-bar hilt design and French-designed blades.

BELOW French Model 1822 Light Cavalry Officer's Sword. Unlike the trooper's version, the hilt has been decorated.

Slightly curved blade

LEFT Falguière's hilt was decorated with patterns of delicate flowing curves and botanical forms around the guard. On the pommel, an open wreath of acanthus and oak foliates surrounds the owner's initials.

French cavalry swords

The Model 1822 Light Cavalry Sword had a long service life, only being replaced in 1896 by a new universal cavalry sword, which served for both light and heavy cavalry. The officer's version of this 1896 Pattern Cavalry Officer's Sword is quite unique with an innovative hilt style. It is very much an example of contemporary Art Nouveau decorative art forms influencing the design of a weapon of war. The hilt ornamentation was designed by the French sculptor and painter Jean Alexandre Falguière (1831–1900), who was a professor at the École des Beaux-Arts in Paris.

Falguière designed the hilt around a pattern of flowing lines and botanical motifs that draped itself around the bowl guard. Symbolism was important to exponents of Art Nouveau (1890s–early 1900s), and we see this with the striking incorporation of the mythological figure of Medusa's head into the curving quillon. The sword has always had an important association in mythology. In this case the designer has focused on the myth of Perseus and Medusa. The sight of the gorgon Medusa would turn men to stone, but Perseus managed to kill her by only viewing her image reflected in his shield. He cut off her head with his sword and gave the head to Athena, who placed it in the middle of her shield to terrify her enemies.

In 1923, a universal model of sword for all officers of the French Army was issued. This was an attractive sword with a gilt-brass, shallow-bowl hilt, and single knuckle bow. The sides of the bowl guard were pierced and decorated with leaf patterns, and its overall appearance was still clearly influenced by the Art Nouveau movement.

ABOVE A professor at the École des Beaux-Arts in Paris, Jean Alexandre Falguière (1831–1900), designed the hilt of the 1896 Pattern Cavalry Officer's Sword in the Art Nouveau style.

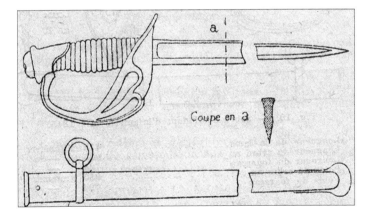

ABOVE An official diagram of the 1896 Pattern Cavalry Trooper's Sword, issued in 1937 by the French Ministry for War.

Naval swords and edged weapons

The truly naval sword probably originated in the 16th or 17th century. Before then, naval officers and sailors carried swords identical to those on land. During this time, navies began to evolve from legalized privateers serving under covert royal patronage into more organized enforcers of a state's military and commercial interests. Ship and crew underwent changes in their administration, equipment and appearance. The emergence of "fighting ships" in the 18th century meant that close hand-to-hand boarding engagements became common. Effective swords, axes and pikes were needed for chaotic, confined naval encounters.

The emergence of the British cutlass

Cutlasses were provided for seamen by the Board of Ordnance. This was a British government authority created in the 15th century with the responsibility for the design, testing and production of armaments for both the British Army and Navy. From the late 1500s, a short-bladed weapon described as a "curtleax", or coute-lace, was carried on British ships. Although this is now thought to have been more of an axe than a sword, the name was established and, by the 18th century, ships' captains began to refer to a specific sword for use on board ship as a "cuttlashe".

British cutlasses in the 18th and 19th centuries

The number of cutlasses carried on board a ship was actually small in relation to the numbers of sailors, and not every seaman was issued with a cutlass. Other weapons such as pikes and axes were employed to fill the gaps. The manufacturing quality of these early cutlasses was quite poor and most cutlass hilts were made from a single piece of thin sheet steel, which opened out into two discs for better hand protection. Blades were flat, single-edged, straight or slightly curved.

Cutlass manufacture for the Royal Navy was undertaken by a number of English sword makers, resulting in a marked variation in both quality and reliability. The official inspection and testing of sword blades was still in its infancy during this period. In 1804, a regulation pattern of seaman's cutlass was adopted.

This was the "figure-of-eight", or double disc-hilted, cutlass and is probably the one most commonly associated with British seamen during the Napoleonic Wars. It comprised a blackened cast-iron hilt with ribbed grip and a straight, flat, unfullered blade.

Subsequent patterns followed in 1814, 1845, 1858 and 1889 until 1900, when the last official pattern was introduced. Naval planners of the 1900s realized that boarding actions in the age of the ironclad battleship were unlikely and no more patterns were introduced after this date. In 1936, the cutlass was withdrawn from British naval use except for ceremonial purposes.

British naval officers' swords in the 17th and 18th centuries

Up until the beginning of the 19th century, a Royal Navy officer was given considerable leeway as to which edged weapons he carried. During the latter part of the 17th century, the rapier was abandoned by naval officers in favour of short-bladed, hunting-type hangers. These short swords were far more practical when officers were fighting amongst the rigging and confined spaces of a ship's deck. Many contemporary portraits show British naval officers carrying these swords. Naval officers might also have carried a smallsword, which was similar in design to those carried by civilians or army officers, although some rare examples displayed nautical motifs to the hilt and blade.

Flat-backed blade

Royal cypher

ABOVE This cutlass, introduced in 1804, became standard issue to the Royal Navy and was carried throughout the Napoleonic Wars.

Quillon

Single-fullered blade

Sword knot

ABOVE British Naval Officer's Sword, *c.*1800. It has a beaded or "five-ball" hilt as well as a "cigar band" (with engraved fouled anchor) to the centre of the grip.

In 1786, the British Army formally adopted a new regulation pattern sword for all infantry officers, and naval officers soon copied this style. The cut-and-thrust blade was straight with a beaded or "five-ball" "D-guard" hilt and cushion pommel. An anchor was also engraved into a gilt-brass "cigar band" that was placed in the centre of a ribbed ivory or ebony grip. Some examples also had a small anchor placed in the centre of a side ring. Other sword types included "S-bar" hilts (which featured an anchor) and stirrup hilts engraved with anchors on each of the hilt langets. These swords imitated contemporary infantry and cavalry swords.

By the late 18th century, the hunting hanger was dropped in favour of a more traditional short infantry sword with "slotted" guard, lion's-head or ovoid pommel and slightly curved blade. To distinguish them from infantry swords, many had a small fouled anchor inserted into the slotted guard or engraved on the pommel.

BELOW A British naval officer's sword, *c.*1815. It has the standard lion's head pommel and the ivory grip indicates that its owner was a high-ranking officer. This is not a fighting sword and would have been carried as a dress weapon, reserved for social occasions.

British naval officers' swords in the 19th century

The 1805 Pattern Naval Officer's Sword was a more recognizably "naval" style of sword. It featured a gilt-brass lion's-head pommel and engraved fouled anchor to the langets (located in the centre of the cross guard). Blades were straight and single-fullered. Many had extensive blue and gilt decoration, including naval motifs such as flags, trophies, anchors and buoys. A Royal Navy midshipman (junior officer) of the early 1800s carried a sword similar in design to senior officers but with black rather that white fishskin or ivory grips. In 1827, officers adopted a solid, gilt-brass, half-basket hilt, a pattern that mirrors the 1822 Pattern Infantry Officer's Sword. The grip was composed of white fishskin (black for warrant officers), and blades were initially of pipeback and quill point profile, changing to a single-fullered "Wilkinson"-type blade in the mid-1850s. The 1827 Pattern is still carried by serving Royal Navy officers today.

Other British naval sword designs included a mameluke sword for flag officers; open rather than solid hilts; "dove-head" pommels (for warrant officers); and a Scottish Highland, or "claymore", blade, which became popular in the late 19th century.

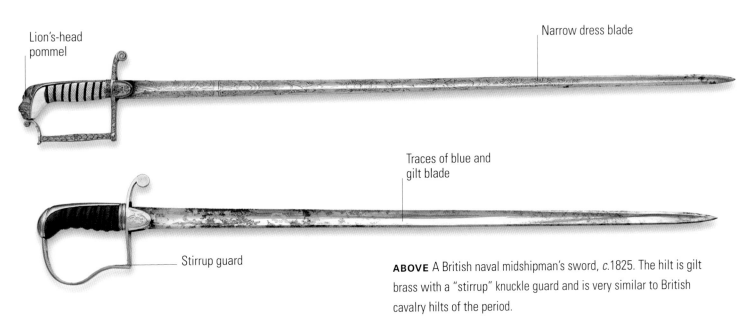

Lion's-head pommel

Narrow dress blade

Traces of blue and gilt blade

Stirrup guard

ABOVE A British naval midshipman's sword, *c.*1825. The hilt is gilt brass with a "stirrup" knuckle guard and is very similar to British cavalry hilts of the period.

Presentation swords

It was common practice during the Napoleonic period for British naval officers to receive presentation swords in honour of their gallant acts in the face of the enemy and bodies such as the Corporation of London regularly bestowed presentation or commemorative swords.

The Lloyds Patriotic Fund presentation swords have since become famous for their opulence, craftsmanship and breathtaking beauty. They were paid for and presented by members of the insurance house, Lloyds of London, between 1803 and 1810, and were given in recognition of the recipient's bravery under fire. They were also an acknowledgement of (and a vote of thanks for) the protection afforded by the Royal Navy to British commercial interests, both home and abroad, during the long wars with Napoleon.

The swords were awarded in four categories depending on the cost of manufacture and rose in magnificence as their value increased. They were presented as swords of £30, £50 and £100 value. There was also a special sword of truly epic grandeur awarded to the 29 captains and lieutenants who commanded ships during the Battle of Trafalgar, in 1805.

The Lloyds' swords had heavy, slightly curved blades with lavishly applied blue and gilt decoration, white ivory grips and opulent hilts of fire gilt. The hilt backpiece was decorated in imitation of a lion skin and the quillons displayed ancient Roman fasces (tied bundles of birch rods wrapped around an axe and symbolizing "strength through unity"). The knuckle guard took the form of a stylized interpretation of the club of Hercules entwined by a serpent. Scabbards were even more elaborate, encased in either leather or blue velvet (depending on the value awarded) and decorated with numerous classical reliefs and panels. The production of these swords was a showcase for the artistry and imagination displayed by some of the finest artisans in Georgian London.

Lion's mane backstrap

Embossed decoration

ABOVE From the Patriotic Fund at Lloyds to Lieutenant James Bowen of HMS *La Loire*, who was commader of one of the boats that successfully attacked a French national brig in 1803.

French cutlasses in the 18th and 19th centuries

In the 18th century, cutlasses in the French Navy were formally standardized with the introduction of a Model 1771 Seaman's Cutlass (modified in 1782-83). The hilt was brass with a ribbed grip and prominent pommel cap. It was similar to contemporary infantry grenadier hilts, but differed in having a three-bar hilt rather than a single knuckle guard.

The Napoleonic Model Year XI (1801–02) Cutlass had a large, half-basket guard of blackened iron, with a smooth octagonal grip and a slightly curved and wide-fullered blade. A later model (1833) saw the addition of an engraved anchor to the blade. The Model 1872 was the last regulation pattern French cutlass and comprised a hilt of plate steel, shaped grip and perforated guard.

French naval officers' swords in the 18th and 19th centuries

During the 18th century, French naval officers followed the British practice of carrying swords similar to those in the army. Later, a more uniform sword was introduced based on a French Light Cavalry Officer's sword differing only in having an engraved anchor within the lozenge-shaped hilt langets. In 1805, a new pattern saw the complete removal of langets and the placing of an anchor within the cross guard.

Curved quillon

Slightly curved,
single-edged blade

In 1837, a completely new sword design is noted. It comprised an elaborately decorated gilt-brass, half-basket hilt, incorporating an anchor, royal crown and display of martial trophies. There followed some slight changes to the hilt decoration in the years 1848 (removal of the royal crown), 1852 and 1870.

ABOVE French Model 1833 Naval Cutlass, with large blackened bowl guard. It evolved from the Year XI Model, 1801–02, Naval Cutlass, introduced during the Napoleonic period.

BELOW Portrait of Louis-Jean-Marie de Bourbon (1725–1793), Admiral of the French fleet. He is carrying a smallsword favoured by officers.

German cutlasses in the 19th and 20th centuries

During the mid-1800s, Prussian naval seamen carried a cutlass that was almost identical to the French Model 1833 Cutlass, differing only in having a distinctive falchion-type blade. It was the standard naval cutlass for the Prussian and, later, the Imperial German Navy throughout the 19th century. In 1911, a new model was introduced that comprised an open steel, three-bar hilt of cavalry type, with a blade similar to contemporary German "butcher"-type bayonets, featuring a gradually widening and double-edged blade.

German naval officers' swords in the 19th and 20th centuries

It is difficult to present an accurate picture of German naval officers' swords before the unification of the country in 1871, as there was no dedicated "German" Navy until the formation of the mainly Prussian Imperial Fleet (Reichsflotte) during the revolutionary period of 1848–52. No tangible attempts were made to standardize sword patterns, and, before 1871, German naval officers carried swords that were similar to contemporary British naval officers' swords, including solid half-basket hilts and lion's-head pommels.

With the establishment of the Kaiserliche Marine, or Imperial Navy, after reunification in 1871, naval officers' swords took on a more specifically "German"

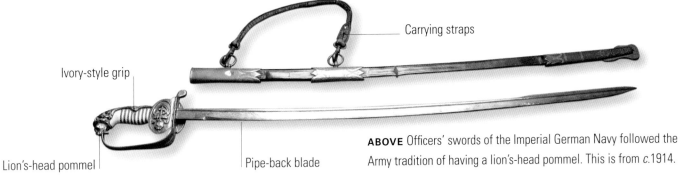

Carrying straps

Ivory-style grip

Lion's-head pommel

Pipe-back blade

ABOVE Officers' swords of the Imperial German Navy followed the Army tradition of having a lion's-head pommel. This is from c.1914.

The boarding pike

For many centuries the simple spear or javelin was a weapon that had been carried on land and at sea. It was only when European nations began to formalize their navies in the 17th and 18th centuries that a designated polearm for boarding ships begin to emerge.

The polearm had many other names, including half pike, strong pike or short pike, and comprised a drastically reduced traditional infantryman's pike. The boarding pike was particularly effective at thrusting and fending off enemies in the confined and restricted spaces of a ship's deck. Pikes were normally kept in racks on board ship.

Early 17th century examples had a pick-style point, square or triangular in cross-section, with long langets, and were designed to deliver a thrusting blow. Later pike heads of the 18th century were more streamlined in profile and so avoided snagging in the rigging of the crowded upper decks of sailing ships. An account by an American, Jacob Nagle, serving on a British sloop of war off the coast of Spain in 1800, gives a dramatic illustration of the primitive effectiveness of a pike when used in trained hands.

In the smoke I purceiv'd the French capt. drawing a pistol from his belt to fire at our capt. that was giving command. I drew a pistol at the same time and let him have the contents. At the same time a stout Frenchman made a blow at me with a large hangar, from the netting, but the man behind me saw the blow and covered my head with his boarding pike, which was cut that it fell and the bare point struck me in the head and I fell, but the man ketch'd up he pike and run it into his body and he fell between two vessels...

from the *Nagle Journal*, 1775–1841, (Weidenfeld & Nicolson, New York, 1988).

BELOW A boarding pike with tomahawk head.

BELOW A boarding pike with spiked point.

style. The solid, gilt-brass hilt and lion's-head pommel remained but became flatter in profile, with the addition of a fold-down guard and Imperial Crown cartouche (a tablet within the hilt). Grips were bone or ivory. This style remained until Germany's defeat in 1918 when the Imperial Crown was removed. During the Nazi period (1933–45), naval officers' dirks, but not swords, bore an eagle and swastika.

Imperial Russia in the 19th and 20th centuries

Like most European navies, Russia did not attempt to formally regulate its naval swords until the 1800s. Russian naval officers of the early 1800s would have carried swords similar to the British 1796 Pattern Infantry Officer's Sword. The 1811 Pattern Naval Officer's Sword set the trend for future Russian naval officers' swords, comprising a brass three-bar hilted sword with a distinctive canted or curved backpiece and pommel. This is a style also found on many French and German military swords of the period. The pattern was updated in 1855 and 1914.

Naval swords remained unchanged until the Russian Revolution of 1917. Thereafter, all Imperial designations to both blade and hilt were erased, and the sword became plainer in design, although some naval officers were known to place Soviet hammer-and-sickle or red-star devices on the blade pommel.

Russian cutlasses

A formal pattern of naval cutlass for Russian seamen was not issued until 1810. Before then, naval ratings carried a short hanger of French "briquet" form. The 1810 Pattern was worn on a shoulder belt and issued to naval bombardiers and gunners. The blade was of Turkish yataghan (forward-curved) style with a brass-hilt cross guard, wooden grip and swollen pommel.

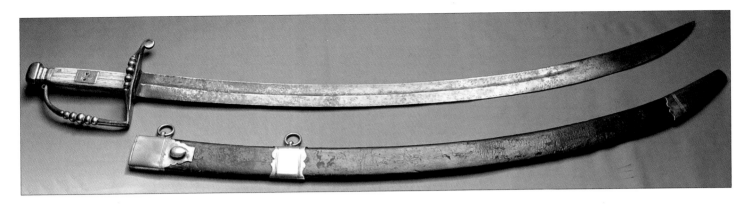

ABOVE An American officer's naval sword from c.1790. The blade is slightly curved and the grip is made from bone.

It was more of a hanger than a cutlass, and did not have the protective bowl guard or disc hilt more commonly associated with European naval cutlasses of this time. The Russian 1856 Pattern Boarding Cutlass was traditionally "western" in style and imitated British and French cutlasses. It had a blackened iron hilt with ribbed grip and matching blackened steel scabbard mounts. Cutlass design remained unchanged until 1940, when a new pattern was introduced for naval cadets. It had a double-edged, slightly curving blade and steel hilt with a pronounced guard and ribbed wooden grip. The need for a cutlass in the 1940s seems rather tenuous, although the Soviet Navy insisted on it being carried when outside the naval school. After 1958, it was only worn on ceremonial occasions.

Russian gallantry swords

Imperial Russian naval presentation swords were very popular in the 19th and early 20th centuries. They differed from standard naval patterns in having solid gilt, ribbed metal grips rather than the usual leather and brass twistwire wrapping. They were known as "Gold Swords" and featured engraved Cyrillic (Russian) lettering (normally with wording such as "For Gallantry") on the hilt bars. A number of grades, or orders, were also presented. An enamelled cross representing either the Order of St George or that of St Anne (before 1869) was also attached to the hilt pommel. Bullion sword knots were worn and their design differed according to the level of order attained.

American naval swords to the 20th century

Both during and after the American Revolutionary War (1775–83), American naval officers carried swords of traditional British or French style. Most were manufactured and exported from these countries to the United States during periods of peace between the two countries. In 1841, an eagle-headed naval officer's sword was introduced and its design closely followed sword styles already prevalent in the army. The Model 1852 Naval Officer's Sword was inspired by European (particularly French) solid, half-basket-hilted naval swords and it is still carried today. Cutlasses of English style were issued in 1797 and 1808.

The Model 1841 and Model 1860 USN cutlasses were both designed by the N.P. Ames sword company of Springfield, Massachusetts. The Model 1841 was derived from contemporary French "gladius" short swords, and the Model 1860 was an interpretation of the French Model AIX (1801–02), albeit with brass hilt and scabbard mounts, rather than the blackened sheet iron used in the French version.

Unusually, there was also an officer's model, differing from the ordinary seaman's cutlass in having the letters "USN" or "US" cut out of the hilt. This cutlass had a long service life and was only replaced in 1917 by a new model based on the Dutch army klewang (machete-style) cutlass. There are two versions: the early model has a solid iron bowl guard while the 1941 variation has a guard with separate branches.

BELOW The Model 1917 cutlass was carried on US Navy ships until the beginning of World War II. It was declared obsolete in 1949.

Bowl guard

Swords of the two World Wars

Despite significant advances in warfare technology during the latter half of the 19th century, including the development of ever-more destructive firearms and artillery, many military commanders entered the first years of the new century still believing that the use of massed cavalry and the flash of steel would easily overcome the new machine guns and rapid-firing rifles. They would be sadly mistaken.

World War I swords

Paradoxically, the very first recorded casualty inflicted by a serving British soldier in Europe during World War I occurred when Captain Charles Hornby of the 4th Royal Irish Dragoon Guards killed a German Uhlan with his sword on 22 August 1914. He was leading a charge against four troopers of the 2nd Kurassier Regiment near the village of Casteau, north of Mons, in Belgium.

Both British and German officers continued to wear swords in the early stages of World War I but it soon became apparent that this was an anachronism totally unsuited to the practicalities of trench warfare. Officers also realized that the carrying of a sword

ABOVE The retreat from Mons during World War I in August to September 1914. Notice that the British cavalry are carrying lances.

The final British cavalry sword of 1908

Probably one of the most radical of all known sword designs is the 1908 Pattern Cavalry Trooper's Sword. It comprised a thin, rapier-like blade, large enclosed bowl-hilt and unique pistol grip. It was as far removed from traditional sword design as could be possible. Its very uniqueness finally resolved the argument within the British military establishment of whether to use a thrusting or cutting blade. The pattern was unashamedly thrusting and designed for the shock of a cavalry charge. The grip was also manufactured in a new composite material, dermatine (the 1912 Pattern Officer's version retained a fishskin covering), and included a thumb depression on the backpiece to enable the carrier to grip the sword in a fashion similar to the gripping of a lance.

Despite the fact that King Edward VII (r.1901–10) described this new design as "hideous", the 1908 Pattern went into full production and was soon standard issue in British cavalry regiments. The advent of World War I (1914–18) was regarded by the military as the ideal testing ground for this new pattern of sword, but the conflict actually sounded its death knell. Confronted with grinding trench warfare and an immovable battlefield typified by the Western Front, the opportunity for massed mobile cavalry action had simply disappeared.

BELOW 1908 Pattern Cavalry Trooper's Sword. Note the solid steel bowl guard and the pistol grip. The blade is rapier-like and designed for thrusting rather than cutting.

Rapier-like blade

Steel bowl guard

Russian cavalry swords

The active use of the sword within cavalry regiments in eastern Europe, and particularly Russia, was still commonplace throughout World War I and well into the 1930s. The vast, open terrain of the Russian landscape was well suited to the use of massed cavalry, and the Russian Cossack troops of both the Czarist and post-Revolutionary Soviet period wielded their favourite shasqua swords (a slightly curved sabre with a single-edged blade) against both German and Bolshevik enemies. The Soviets of the 1920s and 1930s continued issuing swords to Cossack troops (now "integrated" into the Soviet Republic), and these weapons were last called upon during the German invasion of Russia in 1941, when they were recorded as being used by troops undertaking brave but ultimately futile massed attacks against advancing German tanks.

ABOVE Cossack troops charge against German forces in 1942.

made them an obvious and prized target for machine gunners and snipers from both sides. Swords were still purchased but only for dress occasions.

The last massed British cavalry charge was at the Battle of Mughar, near Jerusalem, on 13 November 1917, when a combined force of the Buckinghamshire Hussars, supported by the Dorset and Berkshire Yeomanry Regiments, overran a significant Turkish position, capturing hundreds of prisoners.

British Air Force swords in the 20th century

The 1920s witnessed the emergence of a unique sword for a new branch of the British Army. This was the British 1920 Pattern Royal Air Force Officer's Sword, the last official regulation pattern sword of the British Army. Designed by the Wilkinson Sword Company of London, the hilt was based on the 1897 Pattern Infantry Officer's Sword. This was an acknowledgement of the crucial role played by the Royal Engineers' Balloonist Unit (raised in 1878) in establishing the future Royal Flying Corps (RFC) in 1912 and the Royal Naval Air Service (RNAS) in 1914. They were later merged in 1918 to form the Royal Air Force (RAF). British airmen from the RFC or the RNAS would have originally been posted from different army or naval units, and consequently they would have carried a dress sword appropriate to their original branch of service or regiment. The need for a standardized pattern was therefore obvious. The 1920 Pattern had a gilt-brass, half-basket hilt with eagle-head pommel and crowned winged albatross inset into the hilt cartouche. The grip was white sharkskin. This pattern of ceremonial sword is still carried by serving officers of the RAF.

Italian/German Air Force swords in the 20th century

Both Italy and Germany produced their own air force swords, with both nations drawing heavily on the contemporary Art Deco influences of the 1920s and 1930s. The Italian Air Force officer's sword of the 1930s had a sweeping, gilt brass eagle-head hilt, and the German Model 1934 Air Force Officer's Sword exhibited a very modernistic hilt design, with dramatically downswept quillons and exaggerated pommel.

Nazi swords before World War II

The catastrophic defeat of Germany and its allies in World War I brought a temporary halt to the widespread promotion and wearing of swords in these countries. The size of the German Army during the Weimar Republic (1919–33) was also reduced significantly and the famous German sword-making town of Solingen experienced a drastic reduction in military orders for its edged weapons. Only when the Nazis came to power in 1933 were the fortunes of Solingen reversed. A delegation of officials from the town met the new German Chancellor, Adolf Hitler, and persuaded him that the production of swords and daggers for the Nazi Party (and the armed forces) would create new employment in a town badly hit by the worldwide economic slump of 1929 and the early 1930s (the Great Depression). Soon numerous government and quasi-military organizations within the new Nazi state had adopted edged weapons. The German Army (Heer), Air Force (Luftwaffe) and Navy (Kriegsmarine) all started to carry new sword designs created in the workshops of Solingen.

Japanese swords and polearms

The traditional Japanese Samurai sword is both a devastating weapon of armed combat and an object of great aesthetic beauty. This makes it rather unusual when compared with most military swords, which are primarily functional tools of war. The manufacture of Samurai swords was, for the master swordsmith, part religious ceremony and part spiritual journey. The Samurai warrior, clad in exotic lacquered armour and fearsome horned kabuko helmet, would always ensure that he went into battle armed with a range of swords and daggers, most notably the katana and wakizashi.

Mythical beginnings

The history of the Japanese sword begins with the traditional mythology of Shinto (the native religion of Japan). The Sun Goddess, Amaterasu Omikami, is said to have given her grandson, Ninigi-no Mikoto, a special sword when he was sent down to reign on Earth. The Shinto religion and the worship of the Japanese sword have always been closely linked.

Japanese swords were thought to have miraculous spiritual powers and even a personal identity of their own. Japanese soldiers who were defeated in battle would pray at the shrines of the war god Hachiman, asking why their swords had lost their martial spirit.

This extreme personalization of a Japanese warrior's sword resulted in the application of a strict code of etiquette for the handling and maintenance of swords.

Influence of China and Korea

In historical terms, the origin of the Japanese sword has a timeline of nearly 2,000 years. Japanese sword design mirrored very much the designs in China and Korea during the first two millennia. Swords that have been found in Japanese burial mounds and dated to *c.* AD300 have blades that were long and single-edged, very much like the Chinese jian, with a simple tsuba mount (a disc-shaped swordguard at the end of the handle).

Japanese clansmen warriors from this early period were predominantly horsemen who needed a long-bladed sword that could be used against infantry. Many Japanese swords were actually imported from China and Korea. A truly Japanese home-based sword-making industry only developed later.

The Heian period (AD794–1192)

During the early medieval period, the classic Japanese Samurai sword style started to become more recognizable. This process evolved through the gradual change of the blade shape from straight to slightly curved. During the Heian period, Japanese swordsmiths also began to mark their own work on the blade "tang" (the plate of metal that secures the blade to the sword handle), so enabling future generations to identify both the date of manufacture and the name and province in which the swordsmith lived. The appearance of a more distinctive "hamon", or pattern to the blade, is also evident during this period.

LEFT A 15th-century depiction of a Japanese Samurai warrior carrying sword and polearm. He lived by a code of honour, bravery and loyalty.

RIGHT 19th-century print of a Samurai holding his sword. Note the wakizashi (short sword or side arm) in his belt.

The Heian period, under the direction of Emperor Kammu (AD781–806), produced blades that are regarded as some of the most perfect ever manufactured and they have now acquired an almost mythical status. During this period the Fujiwara class of military nobility began to emerge and adopt this distinctive style of sword.

Other important periods of sword manufacture include the Kamakura period (1192–1333), Shoshino or Namboku Cho period (1333–93), Muromachi period (1338–1573), Edo period (1603–1867) and Showa period (1926–89). These periods relate to dynasties or clans that were based in separate areas of Japan, some at the same time.

The "way of the warrior"

Any history of the Samurai and his association with the sword must first begin with an explanation of bushido, or "the way of the warrior". This was a strict code of behaviour that had to be followed with honour, bravery and utmost loyalty. The Samurai was also taught to live with "freedom without fear". Allied with this moral philosophy was a strong reliance on training in the art of combat (bujutsu).

Early Samurai used a combination of bows and arrows, and swords. Later Samurai used swords, spears and naginata (halberds). Samurai often named their swords as a mark of personal devotion, and believed that their own warrior spirit was actually contained within these swords.

The Kamakura Period (1192–1333)

Samurai warrior culture developed from a series of territorial wars during the Kamakura period amongst the Minamoto, Fujiwara and Taira clans. These feudal groups were constantly at war with each other, and the Samurai (literally meaning "to serve") were drawn from these battle-hardened warriors.

BELOW An 18th-century Samurai sword. Training in its use was complex and required great skill. It was traditionally worn by the Samurai with the blade edge-up.

RIGHT 19th-century print of a Samurai holding his sword. Note the wakizashi (short sword or side arm) in his belt.

This period of Japanese history is viewed as the highpoint of the Samurai warrior, with many stories chronicling their honour, bravery and stoicism in battle. Ironically, this period also allowed the Samurai, as privileged members of society, to kill any unfortunate peasants who offended them. It is also no surprise that some of the best Japanese swords were manufactured during this period.

The Muromachi period (1338–1573)

An interesting period in Samurai history is the Muromachi period, as it witnessed the emergence of the Samurai as an artist-warrior. The culture of the Samurai had now developed to such a degree that it was considered necessary for training to include the ritualized tea ceremony and flower arranging. These rituals were considered to add refinement and balance to the usually warrior-like persona of a Samurai.

Kabuto-gane (pommel)

ABOVE The naginata polearm was commonly used by the Samurai warriors.

Lacquered wood shaft

Blade sharply curved towards point

The decline of the Samurai (1603–1867)

During the Edo period (1603–1867) the gradual decline of the Samurai began. The unusual absence of any wars in Japan during a period of about 250 years meant that the Samurai were unable to play a warlike role in Japanese society. Although they were allowed to wear their traditional swords in public, they now had to accept civilian jobs to survive. The last Shogun, or Governor of Japan, resigned during the Meiji Restoration (1868–1912), and dissatisfied Samurai then led a revolt against a progressive and pro-Western government, which promptly abolished feudalism and in 1871, finally stripped the Samurai of all their special privileges. The carrying of Samurai swords in public had already been outlawed in 1867, resulting in a rapid decline in the number of working swordsmiths.

Changes in sword design in the 19th century

After the demise of the Samurai class in the late 19th century, Japan entered into an unprecedented period of contact with the West. This was reflected by dramatic changes in sword design for regular army forces. Although the traditional Samurai sword was still being made during this period (albeit in very small numbers), military swords from the 1870s to the 1900s were heavily influenced by European designs, most notably the French military. Some Japanese officers' swords were virtual copies of contemporary French military swords.

The Showa period (1926–89)

With the revival of Japanese nationalism during the Showa period, a parallel revival in sword making also occurred. One of the most common Japanese sword styles of the Showa period is the kyu-gunto pattern. It retained the long grip associated with traditional Samurai swords, but had a knuckle bow and pommel of European design. There were many variations of this pattern, including a version for both officers and non-commissioned officers. From the 1920s, when a rebirth of Japanese nationalism brought with it a new-found interest in their Samurai past, many officers reverted back to the classic Samurai sword form. This was the new shin-gunto pattern. Blades were either machine-made or hand-forged, or earlier family or ancestral blades were attached to new hilts. These swords were carried by all branches of the Imperial Japanese Army. Large numbers were destroyed at the end of World War II, but significant quantities were also brought home as souvenirs by the victorious Allied forces.

Indigenous Japanese sword making came to an abrupt end with the defeat of Japan in 1945, but the craft revived again from the 1970s, with great demand for particular swordsmiths.

The naginata polearm

This was a common polearm used by Samurai warriors and is most commonly associated with the Kamakura and Muromachi Periods (1338–1573). The naginata comprised a lacquered (sometimes inlaid with mother-of-pearl) wooden pole approximately 2m (6.5ft) in length. Onto this was forged a curved blade in very much the same way as traditional katana blades – and, indeed, many naginatas were actually mounted with recycled katana blades. The blade, or nakago, of a naginata was secured onto the pole by a single peg, or mekugi.

The yari

A short lance or spear, the Japanese yari was not intended to be thrown in the traditional Western military fashion. It was used by both the Samurai and the common Japanese foot-soldier, or ashigaru. There are many different styles of yari. The two main types are the su yari (straight-bladed) and the kama yari (with horizontal crossbars on the blade).

Lacquered decoration

ABOVE The yari, or short lance or spear, was used by Japanese infantry soldiers and the Samurai.

Types of Japanese edged weapons

There are four main types of Samurai edged weapon.

Tachi (longsword)

This is the original historic sword of the Samurai and had a typical blade length ranging from 60–70cm (23.6–27.5in). It was worn with the blade edge downwards and suspended from a belt with two straps. It was later replaced by the daisho (a combination of the katana and wakizashi worn together) but continued to be worn at ceremonial events and when attending the Imperial Japanese Court. Many tachi were considered important family heirlooms and stored with great care.

Katana (standard sword)

This sword type had an average blade length of over 60cm (23.6in), and was generally used for outdoor combat. The single-edged blade was slightly curved. The sword was developed in the 10th century to accommodate the growing use of Japanese cavalry and was worn hung from the belt, with the cutting edge facing upwards.

Wakizashi (side arm or short sword)

With a blade length of around 30–40cm (11.8–15.7in), this sword was also worn indoors as it provided more ease of movement than the longer katana. Its shorter blade functioned as a side arm, and was well suited for stabbing at close quarters. It was also used to decapitate beaten opponents and take their heads from the battlefield. The traditional Samurai form of ritual suicide (*seppuku*, sometimes known as *hara-kari*, or "cutting the belly") was normally conducted with this type of short sword.

Tanto (short knife)

This is a small knife used in much the same manner as a wakizashi. The average length is 15–30cm (5.9–11.8in). Unlike other traditional Japanese swords that feature a sharpened edge, the tanto was used primarily as a stabbing weapon and was also designed to pierce armour.

Accessories are:

Saya (scabbard)

A Japanese sword is sheathed in a scabbard called a saya, usually made of magnolia wood and lacquered for weatherproofing. A sageo, or length of strong braid, attaches the scabbard to the owner's belt.

Tsuba (guard)

The tsuba is a rounded (sometimes squared) guard placed at the end of the grip of a traditional Japanese sword. The swordsman would place his right index finger on the tsuba to aid his balance and so control the blade more easily.

Tanto

Tsuba

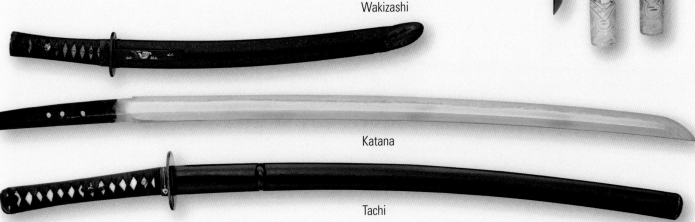

Wakizashi

Katana

Tachi

Chinese and Central Asian swords

The origins of the Chinese sword are rooted in ancient legend. Solid-gold dao swords were reputedly made for the mythical San Huang emperors Fu-Xi-Shi, Shen-Nong-Shi and Sui-Ren-Shi (*c.*3000–2700BC). These swords were said to have extraordinary powers: they could glow in the dark, utter sounds, frighten evil spirits and even change into dragons. Their spiritual powers were embodied in the personal (or perhaps supernatural) strength of their owners. Like Viking swords, these weapons were sometimes accorded individual names.

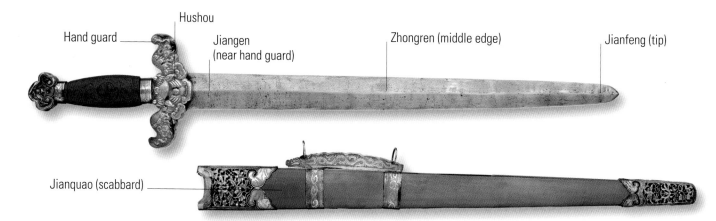

Hand guard — Hushou — Jiangen (near hand guard) — Zhongren (middle edge) — Jianfeng (tip)

Jianquao (scabbard) —

The jian

With a history dating back well over 2,500 years, the oldest type of Chinese sword is the jian. The earliest jian had short, double-edged and straight blades about 35cm (13.8in) in length and were made of bronze. Iron and steel had replaced bronze by the time of the Tang Dynasty (AD618–906), and during the Northern Song Dynasty (AD960–1127) notable jian of high quality were being produced in the Longquan area of Zhejiang province (on China's north-east coast). Raw materials such as iron ore and good access to water helped these swordsmiths to produce very fine blades.

The hilt

A jian hilt comprised a grip of either bound cord, carved wood, horn or wood covered in ray skin (sometimes stained green), with a wide ring or ferrule at each end of the grip. A large, stepped pommel was added for balance. The use of fish skin (normally the rough, dried-out skin of a ray or shark) provided an excellent non-slip surface on which to place a hand. The use of a tassel (a tuft of dyed cotton threads) placed through a hole in the pommel was popular during the Ming Dynasty (1368–1644), and during the Qing Dynasty (1644–1912) a tassel hole was driven through the grip itself.

ABOVE The jian is a straight, double-edged sword used for over 2,500 years in China. The blade itself is normally divided into three sections for use in different techniques of attack and defence.

Hilt fittings were usually made of brass, bronze or silver, and, on rare occasions, gold. Either the hilt was cast as a whole or both the hand guard and pommel were cast separately and then forged together. Decorated sheet metal was also applied to the hilt, and traditional motifs such as dragons and interlaced designs were punched or incised onto the metal.

The blade

A jian blade was divided into three distinct areas. Each had a specific function. The tip of the blade, or jianfeng, had a spear point designed for stabbing and rapid cuts. The middle section was known as the zhongren, and was effective at long cleaving cuts and deflection of the opponent's bade. The last section of blade (closest to the hand guard) was called the jiangen and would have been used for defensive blocking.

The dao – "Marshal of all Weapons"

In China, the dao was regarded as one of the four major Chinese weapons of combat, alongside the qiang (spear), jian (straight sword) and gun (staff

Sabres of the Mongols

When the Mongols invaded China in the early 13th century, they brought with them a curved, one-handed and single-edged cavalry sabre that had been used by Turkic peoples (from central Eurasia) since the 8th century. The curved design of the sabre influenced the shape of the Chinese dao, superseding the straight-bladed jian. During the Ming Dynasty, (1368–1644) sabres of increased curvature appeared, primarily for mounted troops.

RIGHT A 19th-century illustration of the Mongols in China. They are carrying long spears and sabres. Their horsemanship skills and ferocious fighting spirit were greatly feared by the Chinese forces of the Ming Dynasty.

or pole). Described as the "Marshal of all Weapons", it was an effective wide-bladed sword with excellent slashing or chopping capabilities. The word "dao" simply means "knife", and is also used to describe a whole range of single-edged and broad-bladed knives and tools.

Early history

Swords of dao form first emerged during the Shang Dynasty (c.1700–1100BC) and were initially manufactured in bronze, but by the time of the late Warring States (c.221– 5BC) iron and steel would have been utilized by Chinese swordsmiths to produce stronger and more durable blades.

During the Tang Dynasty (AD618–906) of southern China, dao were exported to both Korea and Japan, and became an important influence on the future development of the traditional Japanese Samurai sword, particularly the tachi (long sword) and the katana (standard sword).

BELOW Dao blades have varied greatly over the centuries but most are moderately curved and single-edged. Guards are typically disc-shaped with grips bound in cord.

Characteristics of the dao

Dao blades were broad, slightly curved and single-edged, with canted (angled) hilts, usually bound in cord, leather, wood or ray skin (fish skin). If a dao was to be used in battle, grips would be wrapped in silk, and the colours chosen were specified by strict military regulation. In Chinese culture, the use of particular colours and types of knots was considered to bring their owner luck and bravery.

Most dao had one or more fullers, or "blood grooves", deeply cut into the blade. This would have given the blade extra strength and flexibility. The sword bearer's hand was also protected by a disc-shaped and cupped guard. When the blade entered the scabbard, the "cup" acted as a barrier against rainwater penetrating it, or blood dripping down to the grip and so making the sword difficult to handle. Blade lengths averaged around 65–75cm (25.5–29.5in).

Dao scabbards were usually made of wood, covered with thick lacquer or fish skin, although sometimes they were made from lacquered leather, and many had heavily embossed and gilded panels. The scabbard was mounted with two rings that were attached to a belt.

Disc-shaped and cupped guard

Broad, slightly curved blade

Two-handed swords

Introduced into China around 2,000 years ago, two-handed swords have a long history in Chinese swordsmanship. Although not common, there was a two-handed jian of up to 1.6m (5.2ft) in length. It was known as a shuangshou jian (literally meaning two hands placed together). The dao sword also had a two-handed equivalent, the dadao, or "great sword". This comprised a massive falchion-type blade and simple cord-bound metal hilt with ring pommel. The dadao was used well into the 20th century and there are many photographs showing Chinese Nationalist forces carrying this weapon during the Second Sino-Japanese War (1937–45). Chinese troops boasted that it could sever the head of a Japanese soldier with one blow.

BELOW Emperor Chu Yuan-Chang (1328–98), founder of the Ming Dynasty. During this period the military began to use polearms in favour of the dao sword.

大明太祖高皇帝

Ring-pommelled sword

The eastern Chinese Han Dynasty (AD23–220) adopted a unique type of sword – the single-edged huanshou dao, or "ring-pommelled sword". The blade was quite narrow, with a length of around 90cm (35.4in). The tang was very broad and forged with an integral and distinctive ring pommel. A peg was used to hold both tang and grip together. These ring-pommelled swords were still being used right up until the end of the 19th century. During the Boxer Rising of 1900, these swords were particularly popular amongst the rebel forces who besieged the European contingent in Beijing (Peking).

Polearms and percussive weapons

With the overthrow of the Mongols (or the Yuan Dynasty, 1279–1368) and the establishment of the Ming Dynasty, the Chinese Army began to rely more heavily on the use of long polearms and percussive weapons for their infantry soldiers. In purely economic terms, these weapons were much cheaper to produce and the training required to use them was minimal, unlike the prolonged training necessary to develop a proficient swordsman.

These polearms were still regarded as forms of the dao sword, but in this case the dao blade was attached to a wooden staff or pole. Their names highlight the close relationship they bore to the dao family of swords and included halberds (pointed axes) such as the jidao, and long-bladed glaives (axes) such as the yanyue dao, meijian dao and quadao. In keeping with European military staff weapons of this period, the long reach of the polearm was considered more effective when used by massed infantry formations in battle.

Double or paired swords

In 1644, the last Ming emperor Chung-Chen committed suicide after Beijing (Peking) was captured by the Manchus (from Manchuria, on

Decorative parrying bars or flukes

Axehead

ABOVE This Chinese halberd has a number of defensive bars and a crescent blade. The halberd was used from as early as the Shang Dynasty (c.1700–1100BC) until the end of the Qing Dynasty (1644–1911).

China's eastern seabord). The new emperor Qing Shunzhi, of the Qing (Manchu) Dynasty, did not alter the design of Chinese swords in any radical way, and Ming-style swords, including the traditional jian and dao, continued to be worn until the end of the Qing Dynasty.

However, the Qing Dynasty (1644–1912) did witness the appearance of shuang jian, or paired swords. They are also known as "butterfly knives". These innovative swords were designed in such a way that they fitted back-to-back in the same scabbard and had half hilts that fitted on top of each other. The swordsman could quickly draw these short, double-edged swords out of their scabbard, wielding one in each hand. Hilt and blade design remained similar to the traditional jian.

ABOVE Chinese "Big Sword" troops wield their dao swords during a battle to defend the old Chinese province of Jehol (west of Manchuria) from the attacking Japanese army in March 1933.

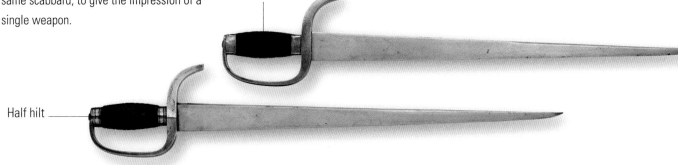

BELOW A pair of butterfly swords. The butterfly sword was usually wielded in pairs. They were held side by side within the same scabbard, to give the impression of a single weapon.

Half hilt

Half hilt

Swords of Tibet

The Tibetan longsword was called the ke tri (pronounced "kay dreh") or patang. These single-edged blades had a short-angled tip with an average blade length of up to 65cm (25.6in). They were usually worn with their edge facing upwards and diagonally across the front of the body, with the hilt located so that the right hand could rest upon it. The sword and scabbard were tucked into a long woollen-fabric waist belt worn with traditional costume. Belt attachments are seldom seen on scabbards. Decoration is quite ornamental, with extensive use of carved turquoise and inlaid coral to the hilt and scabbard. Incised silver work, including filigree (silver wire), is a common decorative feature.

BELOW 19th-century Tibetan longsword. Similar to the Chinese jian, it has a hilt embellished with turquoise and coral and includes an embossed silver scabbard.

Rings for sword belt

Jewelled decoration

African swords

In some African cultures the sword was regarded not merely as a weapon of war but also as an important element in ritual ceremonies. In the hands of a monarch it symbolized divine kingship and power over his subjects. There are great differences in sword design between North Africa, with its distinctively Arabic-inspired swords, and the eastern and Central African empires of the Yoruba, Benin and Asante, where strong beliefs in local spirits encouraged extravagant swords that were symbolic rather than weapons of war.

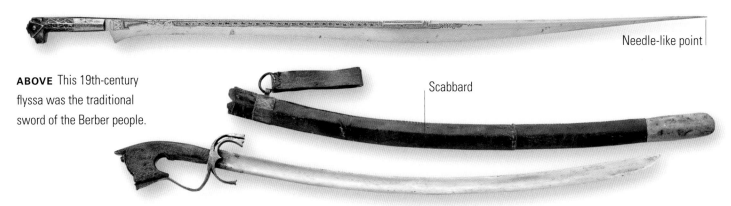

Needle-like point

ABOVE This 19th-century flyssa was the traditional sword of the Berber people.

Scabbard

ABOVE The Moroccan nimcha sword (and scabbard) was often fitted with a European blade.

Swords of North Africa

The influence of the Islamic Arabic world had a profound effect on the indigenous peoples of North Africa. Arab armies began a series of invasions of North Africa after AD600, and with them they brought Islam and new weapons. They introduced both curved and straight-bladed swords over time, some directly influenced by earlier medieval designs, while new hilt and blade forms were developed that became emblematic of distinct regions, peoples and cultures.

The flyssa

This is the traditional sword of the Berber peoples of north-eastern Algeria and parts of Morocco. Swords of this type have single-edged, swelling blades of great length, up to 95cm (37.4in). They feature deeply incised and inlaid brass decoration and pommels of animal heads. The blade point is extremely long and needle-like. This sharp point was effective for piercing chain mail, which was still worn in North Africa well into the 19th century. The flyssa sword grip is without a conventional guard and normally manufactured in iron.

The nimcha

From the 15th century, a unique type of single-handed sword hilt was developed in north-western Africa, especially Morocco. The hilt displayed downward pointing quillons and a wooden or inlaid metal handle with squared-off or "hooked" pommels. From the cross guard, a thin knuckle guard began beneath the quillons and ran to the bottom of the pommel, although not actually joined to it.

Nimcha blades were usually sourced from older, European broadsword blades and many nimcha have Solingen (German), Venetian and Genoese blades from as early as the 17th century. The use of European rather than locally manufactured blades highlights the unique geographical position of this part of North Africa, as it had been an important area of both trade and conflict with the West for many centuries.

The takouba

This sword was used by the nomadic Tuareg tribes of the middle and western Sahara from the 16th century, and is still carried to this day. Up to 1m (3.3ft) in length, the takouba blade is wide and double-edged with three or more hand-ground fullers, or grooves, and a rounded point. The hilt is of simple, cruciform shape. The sword and scabbard are normally worn with a long tasselled baldric (shoulder belt) slung over the right shoulder.

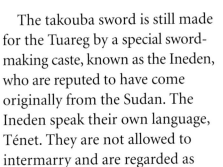

Unfullered blade

The takouba sword is still made for the Tuareg by a special sword-making caste, known as the Ineden, who are reputed to have come originally from the Sudan. The Ineden speak their own language, Ténet. They are not allowed to intermarry and are regarded as having magical powers.

Tassel

Swollen end to scabbard

ABOVE African takouba short sword and scabbard from the nomadic Tuareg tribes of the middle and western Sahara.

Swords of Sudanic West and Central Africa

The ancient empires of the western Sudan and Central Africa (also known as the Sahel) rose to prominence during the medieval period because of the success of their mounted horsemen. Using these horsemen for both raiding and trading parties, they procured large numbers of slaves, gold and ivory from Central Africa, and in return received weapons, most notably swords, spears and lances, from both indigenous peoples and European traders.

The "Crusader" sword

A most distinctive African sword was carried by the Hausa peoples of southern Sudan and northern Nigeria. It comprised a straight, double-edged blade with a cruciform cross guard and disc-shaped pommel. There have been many theories over the years concerning these cruciform-hilted swords, based mainly on the misguided belief that their overtly European and medieval style was introduced into this region by Crusaders of the 12th and 13th centuries.

The kaskara

This sword is readily identified with the Sudan. Blades are double-edged, with a spatulate, or spoon-shaped, tip and a blade length of around 95cm (37.4in). A broad central fuller, or "blood groove", is found on some examples, with others exhibiting multiple fullers. Interestingly, many blades are heavily stamped with spurious European swordsmith marks. Imported European blades were attached to kaskara blades from the 17th and 18th centuries, but most examples still surviving date from the 19th century and these marks were actually added by local sword makers to increase the perceived value and quality of a blade.

The cross guard is usually composed of forged iron although brass examples are also known. It also exhibits a long and thin langet (an extension of the guard). Pommels are of flat, disc form, and the grip is round and normally bound in leather. The 19th-century kaskara sword of the Sultan Ali Diner of Darfur has a hilt of solid gold and the blade is decorated with incised Koranic invocations or prayers.

BELOW A Sudanese kaskara, c.1898, with an Italian blade. This sword was owned by Sultan Ali Dinar of Darfur. It has a highly decorated blade and a gold hilt.

Round pommel

Cruciform cross guard

Multi-fullered blade

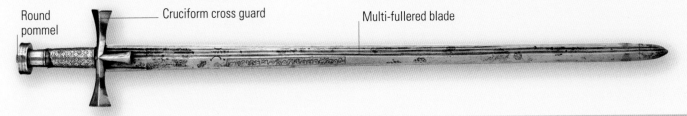

The African blacksmith

In traditional African societies, the blacksmith is still widely regarded as a figure of mystery and magic, possessed of supernatural powers. As such, he is considered ethnically distinct.

His mythology and status can be traced back to the acquisition by sub-Saharan blacksmiths of the knowledge to work iron. This probably derived from ancient Egypt and moved steadily southwards, so that by the 3rd and 4th centuries BC, iron was being worked in north-western Tanzania, northern Nigeria and the Sudan.

There was no Bronze Age in Africa; therefore, the blacksmiths' leap from producing stone and wood tools and weapons to iron must have seemed revolutionary (even supernatural).

A blacksmith's appearance in a village would initiate great excitement. A forge was set up and he would use a stone or iron anvil, iron tongs, bellows of

stitched animal skins and clay tubes to funnel air to stimulate the fire. He produced a range of weapons, most notably daggers, swords and spearheads. The scarcity of reliable, durable weapons to subjugate rival tribes made him a revered figure. He would also manufacture agricultural tools to help sustain the village in more peaceful periods.

RIGHT These 18th–19th-century iron-bladed swords with wooden handles were characteristic of the weapons made by local blacksmiths.

Swords of eastern Africa

Originating in Abyssinia (ancient Ethiopia), the shotel is an extremely curved sword that is very reminiscent of a large sickle. The blade is diamond-sectioned and usually flat-backed or with a central ridge. The blade length is about 80cm (31.5in) and the wooden hilt is simple, smooth and undecorated. There is no guard. This sword would have been carried in a close-fitting leather scabbard.

Shotel swords were not very practical for slashing an opponent, but the extremely curved blade was used primarily to hook the enemy by reaching around his shield and then stabbing him in vital areas, such as the kidneys, heart or lungs.

Swords of West Africa

By AD900 the Yoruba people, originally located in central Nigeria, had slowly begun to move southwest. This was a reaction to northern Hausa expansion southwards into

their lands, combined with long periods of devastating drought. The Yoruba finally settled in an area now comprising south-west Nigeria, Benin and Togo. They were noted swordsmiths and were involved in the mining and smelting of iron ore before AD800.

Yoruba and Edo swords

Between 1100 and 1700, the Yoruba kingdom of Ife flourished in conjunction with the neighbouring Edo kingdom of Benin, and part of this cultural cross-fertilization saw the introduction of the ada sword. This was an all-iron longsword (used either one-handed or double-handed), with a narrow and then greatly widening leaf-shaped and double-edged blade, designed for hacking and cutting. The oral tradition of the Edo people says that the ada sword was used primarily for ceremonial purposes and it would have been presented to the early rulers of Benin. They were known as the Ogiso, or "rulers of the sky".

RIGHT The shotel – the traditional curved sword of Ethiopia. This particular weapon was presented to Benito Mussolini following Italy's conquest of Abyssinia (Ethiopia) in 1936.

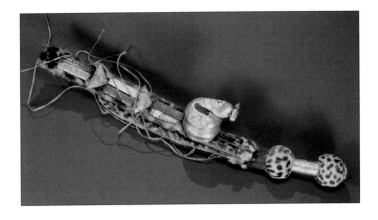

RIGHT An Asante oath-taking sword or mponponsuo from Ghana, with a gold and leopard skin handle.

RIGHT An Asante oath-taking sword or mponponsuo from Ghana, with a gold and leopard skin handle.

In the 15th and 16th centuries, when Yoruba kings, or Obas, had taken over the rule of Benin, the ordinary soldier began to carry a short sword called an opia. This was a double-edged and smaller version of the ada. Benin tribal chiefs carried a specific sword called an eben. It was seen as a symbol of authority and comprised a broad blade with looped handles, elaborately decorated with openwork and brass inlays. If a neighbouring kingdom was at war with Benin and captured a Benin blacksmith, he would not automatically be executed (which was the usual fate for ordinary warriors). His metalworking skills were highly prized and he would quickly be put to use producing tools and weapons for his captors.

Asante state swords

The empire of the Asante (a federation of Akan-speaking and neighbouring tribes) was located in present-day Ghana. During the mid-18th century its influence began to replace that of the Benin empire. The Asante's divine king, or Ansantehene, was given a state sword, or afena. This was recognized as the

ABOVE Dating probably from the 17th century, this bronze plaque from Benin depicts the Oba of Benin with attendants.

supreme symbol of kingly power. The iron blade was curved, with a broad point gradually tapering towards the tang where a hilt of wood was covered in gold. The rounded grip expanded into a sphere at both ends. On both the hilt and the sheath there were a number of elaborate gold castings called abosodee. They had great symbolic importance and represented complex stories within the culture of the Asante kingdom. The decoration included grotesque human heads, knots, shells, fighting warriors and fantastical creatures.

There were also a number of derivations of the afena sword. These included the asomfofena. This would be carried by representatives of the Asantehene (king), whose primary role would be to disseminate the king's will throughout the land. If an Asante was in the presence of this sword, he would know that the royal bearer deserved great respect and that the judgement of the king imparted through this instrument of the state could have both benign and fearful consequences.

The "keteanofena" was a term used to describe a group of important Asante state swords. The akrafena sword was associated with the religious and spiritual well-being of the community and was always carried on the right side during official processions. The bosomfena represented political and secular authority and would be carried on the left during official processions. The mponponsuo was the largest of the state swords and it was used to swear allegiance to the king. The bosommuru was used to swear allegiance to the Asante nation.

The afenatene was a most unusual ceremonial sword that comprised three widening blades that splayed outwards. The blade had a cut-out of fretwork decoration with animal motifs. The long iron shaft sometimes represented the body of a snake, links of a chain, or a series of complex, entwined knots. This sword would have been placed behind the king as he sat in state in his palace at Kumase, in present-day Ghana.

Indian swords

Distinguished by the sheer variety and uniqueness of their design, Indian swords are totally unlike Western swords. They reveal a strong visual extravagance that perfectly mirrors the huge size of the Indian subcontinent and its diffuse melting pot of cultural influences. From the Arabic-inspired north Indian talwar, sword of the Mughal princes, to the European-bladed south Indian firangi, or "foreign" sword, Indian sword makers were constantly producing weapons to amaze and instil terror in their enemies.

Downward-curving cross guard

Double-edged yelman

Jade hilt

The Indian dynasties

From around 180BC, ancient Hindu India experienced a number of invasions from Central Asia. The Indo-Parthians (from the area now known as Afghanistan), the Kushans (from what is now Tajikstan, Afghanistan and Pakistan), the Scythians (from Central Asia) and

ABOVE An Indian sword of the Mughal era, 1526–1857, when most of the Indian subcontinent was ruled by a dynasty founded by the Mongol conqueror, Babur. The jade hilt is decorated with rubies.

even the Greeks (under Alexander the Great) all established either kingdoms or strong cultural influences, particularly in northern India.

The Maurya Empire (184BC–c. AD320) drove out these foreign invaders, and their pan-religious empire stretched from the Himalayas in the far north to the extreme southern Indian provinces of what are now Karnataka and Kerala. By the early 4th century AD, India had experienced a series of devastating internal wars, and, despite another period of internal unity (under the Gupta Dynasty, AD320–c.550), dynastic wars continued for the next few hundred years.

Militarily, however, the Indian subcontinent appears to have lagged somewhat behind the West and it is interesting to note that iron weapons did not appear in India until c.500BC. The sword was not even regarded as an important weapon and infantry were largely composed of bowmen. India's greatest military treatise, the *Siva-Dhanur-Veda* (c.500BC), concentrated on describing the important role of archers and their bows and arrows, to the detriment of any other bladed weapons.

To explain this anomaly, we must first consider the benign influence of Hindu religious culture in the conduct of war. Hand-to-hand conflict was usually avoided, as was mass slaughter. Nevertheless, despite

ABOVE Indian troops depicted using curved talwars against the English at Khurkowhah, 15 August 1857, during the Indian Mutiny.

Members of Indian royalty of the 19th century would have carried swords of great artistry and value.

the constraints imposed by religious beliefs, some astonishing edged weapons would be produced in the following centuries.

During the 11th and 12th centuries, India witnessed continuous and devastating invasions from Muslim Turks, Arabs and Afghans. In 1206 the Mamluk Dynasty (the first Muslim dynasty) was established, and there followed three centuries of Muslim rule throughout northern India. The south of the continent was not affected by this Muslim invasion and remained independent under the Hindu Vijayanagara Dynasty (1336–1646). In 1526, Babur Timurid, a Central Asian emperor and descendant of Genghis Khan, established the highly influential Mughal Empire (1526–1857), which reigned successfully over most of India and Afghanistan until its dissolution under British rule in the 19th century following the Indian Mutiny of 1857–58.

The British Raj

During the late 18th and early 19th centuries, the British East India Company had extended its control over most of India, paving the way for the establishment of the British Raj. These political changes had a limited impact on Indian swordsmiths, who continued to produce swords in a great diversity of forms. These included not only mainstream swords in the Muslim and Hindu traditions, such as the talwar and the khanda made for the princely states that survived under British rule, but also many regional or tribal variants.

The talwar

One of the most common of Indian swords, the origins of the talwar (*war*, or *vaar*, means "strike", as in "strike a blow") can be traced back to Central Asian invaders (the Saka-Jushans, ancestors of the Turks) who established their kingdoms in north-western

India during the 13th century. They brought with them a curved sword of scimitar shape which was soon adopted by the indigenous Indian warrior clans, ancestors of the future Rajputs (a Hindu warrior dynasty, c. AD700–1947, originally from Rajasthan, a north Indian region bordering present-day Pakistan).

The all-metal talwar includes a disc pommel and a curved knuckle bow of inverted S-shape that is a continuation of the cross guard but does not actually attach itself to the pommel. Hilt quillons are usually globulous (rounded) and the middle part of the knuckle bow splays outwards towards the blade, forming pointed langets (the central area of the cross guard).

Scabbards are normally made of wood with leather or bright velvet covering.

BELOW This Indian talwar sword from the late 18th or early 19th century is all steel. Typically, it has a curved blade of up to 76cm (30in) and a disc-shaped pommel. It was used for slashing and thrusting.

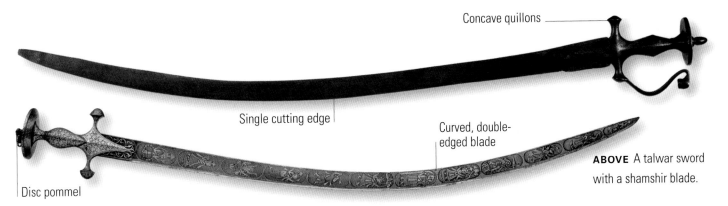

Concave quillons

Single cutting edge

Curved, double-edged blade

ABOVE A talwar sword with a shamshir blade.

Disc pommel

Although plain hilts were common, especially for the ordinary infantry soldier, many talwar hilts were decorated with ornate designs, including intricate chiselling or exquisite gilding. This gilding was done by a process called kofgari (meaning "goldbeating") or damascening (the complex inlaying of steel and gold). Hilts made for local rulers and people of rank are found with superb enamelling and inset jewels. Decoration was not just limited to the hilt. Blades were also decorated with fine incising (metal carving) or damascening.

BELOW An Indian presentation sword dated 1847, made for Henry Hardinge, Governor General of India, 1844–48. It was most likely produced by Indian craftsmen in Lahore.

Persian talwar blades

In the medieval period, blades made in Persia (modern-day Iran) were highly prized in India. Persian swordsmiths were recognized as being masters of the complex process of blade pattern welding. This involved the continuous hammering, twisting and folding of the blade to produce not only a very hard and durable weapon but also one that exhibited a finely textured and patterned surface.

The "forty steps"

One specific pattern that was held to be superior to all others was known as the Ladder of the Prophet, or kirk nardaban (forty steps). It was a highly skilled effect and exhibited an application of a number of decorative chevrons, or stripes, down the blade. The bidr or qum (gravel) effect was another type of patterning applied to the blades of talwar swords.

Indian-made talwar blades

By the 16th century, the supply of blades from Persia and Damascus (Syria) had virtually dried up, and so Indian swordsmiths had to start producing their own work rather than rely solely on imported blades. They did this by introducing their own unique patterned steel, known as wootz (meaning "steel" in some south Indian languages). Importantly, the production of wootz blades replaced the time-consuming method of folding and hammering the steel. This was because the local iron ore naturally produced crystallized structures in the steel that local craftsmen were able to enhance by simple polishing.

Talwar blade marking

Blades of high quality were invariably marked by their makers in the form of a cartouche or tablet in the area just below the hilt (the forte). A gilded bedouh, or

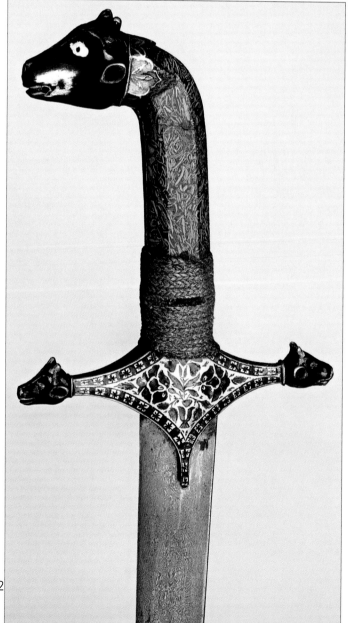

LEFT An 18th-century Indian shamshir from Jaipur. The ends of the quillons and the pommel are modelled as animals' heads, which have been coated with blue enamel.

square, was also applied to this part of the blade and then divided into four quarters, each quarter displaying one of the Arabic numerals for the numbers 2, 4, 6 and 8. These numbers were thought to bring good fortune to the sword's owner.

Rounded cartouches inlaid in gold and carrying invocations or prayers from the Koran were also added. Another decoration that is common to many Indian swords is bidri, a combination of black-stained pewter and silver. This produced a dramatic contrasting effect. Bidri decoration originated in the city of Bider, northwest of Hyderabad (now capital of the present-day southern Indian state of Andhura Pradesh).

The talwar in battle

Being a curved sword, the talwar was useful when striking against bone or armour because it would not easily become embedded, as in the case of straight blades. The Rajput horsemen had a fearsome reputation for wildly attacking infantry formations, and, at close quarters, the short, spiked end on some talwars was efficient at stabbing an opponent in his face if unprotected.

The talwar in Indian culture

An extremely important symbol of Rajput traditions and customs, the talwar sword also became an inseparable part of their culture. It was used to bestow honours and titles to tribal chiefs and it symbolized prestige and honour. In the case of a groom being unable to attend his own wedding due to illness, his personal talwar sword could be sent along to take his place and so enable the wedding rituals to continue without him.

An oath of allegiance to a tribal clan was also sworn on a talwar sword by Rajput warriors. It comprised the words *dhal talwar ki aan* ("by the honour of my sword and shield").

BELOW By the 16th century, the supply of superior blades from Persia and Damascus had virtually ceased. In response, Indian swordsmiths produced their own patterned blades. This Persian sword would have been made with Damascus steel.

ABOVE A mid-17th-century Indian miniature from Bijapur showing a warrior with talwar and pata, or gauntlet sword.

Afghan pulwar or talwar

Due to the talwar's growing popularity within the Mughal Empire, its influence spread northwards, and its design was interpreted by Afghan warriors who produced their own version, the Afghani talwar, or pulwar. Despite this acceptance of an "enemy's" sword, the Afghan and Rajput regions were constantly at war with each other, and contemporary Rajput texts frequently state how "…the Afghan army's sword broke under the Rajput talwar."

Unsharpened edge | Inlaid gold decoration

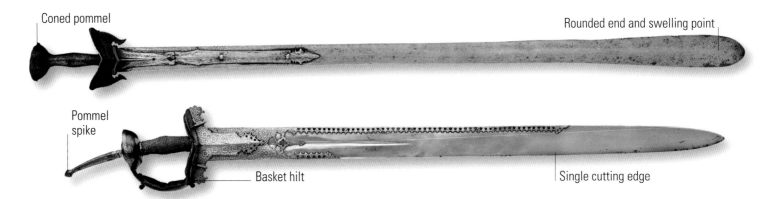

Coned pommel

Rounded end and swelling point

Pommel spike

Basket hilt

Single cutting edge

The khanda

It is thought that the origins of the khanda can be traced back to the Gupta Dynasty (AD320–550), as khanda-type swords have been recognized on period sculptures. During the medieval period, Rajput kings are depicted in wall paintings wielding this type of sword. The name "khanda" is thought to originate in the Sanskrit word for sword, *khanda*.

The khanda has a distinctive, wide and straight, watered steel (pattern-welded) blade that widens towards a spear-pointed tip. A light, flexible blade is characteristic of the khanda, as are two stiffened, ribbed reinforcements that run alongside the blade edge on either side; one is almost the length of the blade and the other is much shorter, to allow a cutting edge. This reinforcement produced a much lighter sword, having greater manoeuvrability than a thick, heavy blade.

TOP A khanda sword from around 1800 with a light and flexible spatulate blade, from Malabar in south-west India. It has a reinforcement bar that runs part of the way down the blade.

ABOVE Late 18th-century khanda sword with a typical Hindu basket hilt. It has a pronounced spiked pommel which was used if the swordsman needed a two-handed grip.

The khanda's hilt and pommel are similar to firangi swords, but with the addition of a wide, disc-like cross guard and knuckle bow. The hilt is also more basket-like in form than other open-hilted Indian swords. The long, spiked and canted (slightly curved) pommel that is found on khandas is thought to have a double use, both producing a double-handed option and acting as a handy walking stick (when unsheathed) or hand rest (when sheathed).

The pata (gauntlet sword)

One of the most unusual of Indian edged weapons, the pata comprises a long, straight-bladed and doubled-edged sword attached to an armoured, half-gauntlet hilt. The overall length could be up to 110cm (44in). In order to wield the sword effectively, the wearer gripped a concealed cross bar inside the gauntlet. Pata swords were favourite weapons of the southern and central Indian Maharatta Empire. The extended grip provided by the encasing

of the forearm also allowed the user a very powerful, sweeping blow. Some warriors chose to carry a pata on each hand and would adopt the stance of a whirling windmill as they attacked swathes of infantry or even armoured cavalry.

Shivaji Bhosle (1627–80), founder of the Maharatta Empire, was known to be a practised exponent of this sword. It is said that one of his famous generals, Tanaji Malusare, wielded a pata in each hand during the Battle of Sinhagad (1670), a now legendary encounter between the Marathas and Mughal forces besieged in a hilltop fort, near Pune (the present-day western Indian state of Maharashtra).

BELOW Indian pata, 18th century. It was considered a highly effective weapon for the infantry and also used against armoured cavalry.

Gauntlet

Straight, double-edged blade

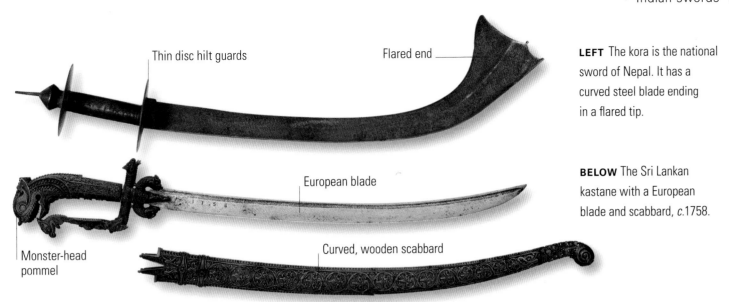

Thin disc hilt guards

Flared end

LEFT The kora is the national sword of Nepal. It has a curved steel blade ending in a flared tip.

European blade

BELOW The Sri Lankan kastane with a European blade and scabbard, *c.*1758.

Monster-head pommel

Curved, wooden scabbard

Weapon of last resort

To a Rajput horseman, the khanda was very much a lethal weapon of last resort. If unhorsed and surrounded by the enemy, he would quickly draw the large blade and begin swinging it around his head, taking full advantage of its estimable hacking and slashing functions. Because of the great width of the khanda blade, it was never perceived as an efficient thrusting sword.

The khanda was effective against the leather and chain-mail armour of the Mughal invaders, as its great strength (especially when wielded with two hands) could cut through these materials with considerable ease. When carried by infantrymen, this sword gave them a chance against horse-mounted soldiers.

The firangi

This was a typical sword of the Hindu southern and central Indian Maharatta Empire (1674–1818). The firangi had a narrow, straight blade, commonly made from imported European blades (the word "firangi" literally means "foreigner") and sometimes decorated with kofgari-worked inlaid gold or silver. When it was fitted with a home-made blade, it was called a sukhela, and in the Deccan (comprising the south Indian plateau), a dhup.

Like the khanda, the firangi blade is also reinforced along the blade edge, combined with a disc-shaped pommel terminating in a long spike used for a two-handed blow. Kofgari or inlaid gold ornamentation frequently decorated the hilt. The large, basket-type hilt is also padded and embroidered with silk or coloured velvet. In the 17th and 18th centuries, the Maharattas of the Western Deccan relied heavily on imported European trade goods and especially sword blades. The Maharattas' preference was for German and Italian blades, since they regarded English blades as very inferior.

The shamshir

Translated literally as "curved like a lion's tail", the shamshir was a distinctively curved sword introduced into India during the 16th century. Persian (Iranian) in origin, its fine pattern-welded or watered blades are some of the finest blades ever to have been produced.

The kora

Nepalese edged weapons were strongly influenced by the medieval Indian Rajputs, who brought Indian weapon styles into the region. Alongside the legendary kukri knife (a heavily curved tool and weapon), the kora is the traditional weapon of the Gurkhas (from Nepal and northern India). Its simple all-metal design comprises a wide and heavy blade with a massive flared tip. The grip was tubular, including a thin, disc-shaped pommel and cross guard. Decoration of koras includes chiselling and mounting of precious metals to the hilt.

The kastane

Sri Lanka's national sword, this distinctive weapon has a short, flat-backed or unfullered blade. The hilt is usually highly ornamented and includes fantastical creatures located at the end of multiple quillons. Gold and silver decoration is richly applied throughout, including the blade, where gilt damascening is worked for most of its length. European blades were frequently mounted on kastane hilts of the 17th and 18th centuries, highlighting the strong commercial ties with the West, particularly Portugal, which established successful trading bases in the country.

Index